ONE FOR THE ROAD

Max Hodes is an award-winning columnist
with the *Scottish Daily Record*.

His Futura titles include *The Official Scottish
Jokebook* – the most borrowed title in
Aberdeen Public Library – and *The World's
Worst Joke Book*, described by the critics as
'unpickupable'.

He dedicates this sparkling collection of
drinking jokes to his wife, who never lets him
get drunk at a party. She always beats him to
the punch.

MAX HODES

ONE FOR THE ROAD

A [Futura] Book

First published in 1986
by Futura Publications, a Division of
Macdonald & Co. (Publishers) Ltd.
London & Sydney

ISBN 0 7088 3013 7

Photoset in North Wales by
Derek Doyle & Associates, Mold, Clwyd
Printed in Great Britain by
Collins, Glasgow

Futura Publications
A Division of
Macdonald & Co (Publishers) Ltd
Maxwell House
74 Worship Street
London EC2A 2EN

A BPCC plc Company

This chap came into the pub with a crocodile on a lead. 'Do you serve Millwall supporters?' he asked.

'No problem,' replied the barman.

'What'll you have?'

'A pint of bitter for me and a Millwall supporter for the crocodile.'

Man in pub: 'Can I have that drink they advertize on TV?'

Barman: 'Which one's that, sir?'

Man: 'You know – the one they spill over Joan Collins.'

'What's that you're busy building?' Charlie asked his pal.

'I'm trying to make a case for beer.'

'You don't have to – I'm convinced.'

Notice in bar: 'The trouble with telling a good story is that it nearly always reminds the other fellow of a bad one.'

Murphy strolled into a pub and ordered eighteen pints of Guinness. 'Why so many?' asked his pal.

'Can't you see the sign?' said Murphy.

' "Nobody served under eighteen." '

1st drunk: 'Do you know what time it is?'
2nd drunk: 'Yes.'
1st drunk: 'Thanks.'

One night in the pub a stranger offered to buy the mother-in-law a double gin and tonic. She felt really insulted. But she managed to swallow the insult.

A fellow wandered into a bar with a LONG VEHICLE sign. Asked where he got it, he explained it fell off the back of a lorry.

I always feel sorry for people who don't drink. Because, when they wake up in the morning, that's the best they're going to feel all day.

Sign outside a Belfast pub: BOOZNESS AS USUAL.

This holidaymaker dashes into the country pub. 'Help,' he shouts, 'my mother-in-law has sunk up to her ankles in the bog on the moors.'

'Don't worry,' says one of the locals, 'let me finish this pint and then I'll help you pull her out.'

'Thanks,' says the holidaymaker, 'I'll have a pint while I'm waiting.'

'Right, then,' says the local, draining his glass, 'I don't think she'll be in much further than her knees by now.'

'I'm not so sure,' says the holidaymaker, 'I forgot to mention she was in head first.'

What is a Scotsman's favourite drink?
    The next one.

The doctor examined newly-wed Arthur.
    'What seems to be the trouble?' he asked.
    'I feel so weak, doctor,' came the reply. 'Last night in the pub I threw a dart ... and went with it.'

Sign in bar: 'If you drink like a fish, please swim home.'

An Englishman on holiday in Cork went into a bar and overheard an old man and a young

7

chap talking.

'That's a fine hat you've got there,' said the old fellow. 'Where did you buy it?'

'I got it at O'Grady's,' replied the young man.

'Why, I go there myself,' said the man. 'You must be from around these parts?'

'That's right,' came the reply. 'I live in Connemara Street.'

'That's amazing,' said the old man. 'I happen to live there, too.'

At this point, the Englishman turned to the barman and said: 'It's a small world. Those two over there live in the same street and have only just met.'

'Don't you believe it,' said the barman. 'They're father and son – but they're always too drunk to recognize each other!'

How about the drunk who got a phone call from the blood bank to say his blood had bounced?

Pub graffiti: COUNT DRACULA – YOUR BLOODY MARY IS READY.

PubTalkPubTalkPubTalkPubTalkPubTalk

'Lazy? He's been off work for six months with a broken flask.'

'How's your headache, Dave?'
  'Out playing Bingo.'

'Hey, Jimmy, what would you do if you broke your arm in two places?'
  'I wouldn't go in those two places again.'

'Pills habit-forming? Rubbish! I've been taking them every night for twenty years.'

'The wife isn't herself tonight. Have you noticed the improvement?'

'It's terrible trying to bring up a family today, what with the price of drink.'

'Do you drink Guinness, Sean?'
  'Well, what else can you do with it?'

'Archie, I think I'm drunk. Help me fall over, will you?'

Sign in bar: 'We have a special arrangement with the bank. They don't serve beer and we don't cash cheques.'

This dwarf in a pub is reaching for a pint, when a big feller comes in and thumps him. 'What did you hit me with?' asks the dwarf when he comes round.
  'A Burmese karate chop to the throat,' replies the big chap.

9

So the dwarf goes out, comes back with a ladder, and hits the big man on the back of the neck.

When he recovers, he rubs his neck and asks: 'What the hell was that?'

And the dwarf says: 'A Morris Oxford starting handle.'

Then there was the boozer who gave up drinking for the sake of his wife and kidneys.

A drunk saw a nun trying to cross the street, so he stopped the traffic and helped her over.

'Thanks very much, my good man,' said the nun.

'Tha'sh all right,' replied the drunk. 'Any friend of Batman ish a friend of mine.'

Pub graffiti: KEEP TAKING THE PILS.

Three sales reps were having a pub lunch. 'I'll pay,' says one. 'With income tax as it is, it will only cost me half.'

'No, I'll get it,' says another. 'It'll come out of repairs and cost me nothing.'

'This is on me,' says the third. 'I work on a cost-plus basis, and this will show me a profit.'

On a T-shirt in a pub: I DON'T HAVE A DRINKING PROBLEM. I DRINK, GET DRUNK AND FALL DOWN. NO PROBLEM!

'A steak and kiddly pie, please, barman.'
  'You mean steak and KIDNEY, sir.'
  'I said kiddly, diddle I?'

This champion boozer staggered out of the pub one night and wandered around for hours looking for his house. Finally, he waved down a taxi. 'Take me to 95 Grantley Avenue,' he asked the driver.

'Are you joking?' said the driver. 'You're outside 95 Grantley Avenue.'

'All right,' said the boozer, reaching for his money. 'But, next time, don't drive so bloody fast!'

Pub graffiti: IF YOU NEED A HELPING HAND, THERE'S ONE ON THE END OF YOUR BODY.

A friend of Tommy's was having a pint in his local when another chap came in.

'Bert Cassidy!' says Tommy. 'I haven't seen you in years. How you've changed! You used to weigh 22 stone and now you're thin. You used to have a great thatch of hair and now you're bald. You used to have a beard and now you're clean shaven.'

The other fellow looked at him. 'My name isn't Bert Cassidy,' he said.

'Fancy that,' said Tommy. 'You've changed your name as well!'

Heard about the Aberdonian who drinks Scotch and Horlicks? When it's his turn to pay, he's fast asleep.

Sign outside pub: 'No admittance unless you want to come in.'

A policeman saw a little boy standing in a pub, smoking a cigarette and drinking a pint of beer. 'Why aren't you in school?' he asked.

Replied the boy: 'Because I'm only four years old.'

A man took his dog into a pub. When the soccer scores came on the telly and it was announced Fulham had lost, the dog went mad, knocking over tables and attacking customers.

'What's got into your dog?' asked the barman.

'He just can't take it when Fulham are beaten.'

'What does he do when they win?'

'I dunno – I've only had him nine months.'

Car sticker: CHARTERED ALCOHOLIC.

Two drunks in a bar. One excused himself and left. 'Where were you?' asked the other on his return.

'I went to the men's room.'

'Will you go for me?'

'OK.'

Two minutes later, the drunk comes back.

'Did you go for me?' asked the other.

'Sure, but I've news for you. You didn't need to go.'

Man in pub: 'We're having separate holidays this year. I'm papering the upstairs bedroom and she's painting the kitchen.'

PubTalkPubTalkPubTalkPubTalkPubTalk

'How far do the strippers go?'

'Two of them go as far as Huddersfield.'

'This turn's been thrown off more stages than John Wayne.'

'Tell me – why do you knock back your drinks one after the other like that?'
  'I once had one stolen.'

'Where's Rodger disappeared to?'
  'Oh, he'll be back in a couple of shakes.'

'The best feature of the wife's cooking is that she serves small portions.'

'Yes, the dog's house-trained. He does it in the house.'

'If there's life after death, I hope I come back as a sponge.'

'The lads call him Vic, because he gets up everyone's nose.'

IRISH PUB GRUB

Soup du Jour 40p
  Soup du Yesterjour 20p
  Pig's Head, English style (brains removed) £3
  Shiska Bog £1.50
  Potatoes baked in their donkey jackets 25p
  Lager with lime (by the shovelful) 65p
  Swiss cheese with holes 85p

Extra portion of holes 30p

Customers who pay for their meal and leave without eating will be prosecuted.

Never tell a Scotsman who's tight to hang loose.

Car sticker: 'Don't drink too much on New Year's Eve. I will accompany you free of charge and drink too much for you.'

Three Welshmen in a pub.

'Best glass of beer I never tasted – no better.'

'So did I neither.'

'Neither did I too.'

How about the man who poured beer on his grass so it would come up half cut?

This punter won £150 on the Derby and headed straight for his local. Next morning, he woke up in bed, £150 poorer and his mind a blank. He raced back to the pub.

'Tell me,' he asked the barman, 'was I in here last night?'

'You sure were,' came the reply. 'You stood

drinks all round and we all had a hell of a time.'

'Thank God for that,' said the punter. 'For a minute I thought I'd squandered it!'

Charlie, a compulsive boozer, was saved from drowning on holiday, and was telling his wife about it.

'It was terrible, love, terrible,' he said. 'I must have swallowed at least a gallon of water.'

'Never mind,' consoled his wife, 'at least now you know what the stuff tastes like.'

A chap came home from the pub one night and found his wife with two black eyes. 'Where did you get the shiners?' he asked.

She said: 'The lodger gave them to me ... he's upstairs.'

So the chap shouted up: 'Hey – did you give my wife two black eyes?'

'That's right,' said the lodger.

'What the hell for?'

'I found out she was unfaithful to us.'

Heard about the pilot who bumped into a bollard as he was leaving the pub? The doctor said he had an airline fracture.

Pub notice: 'Players picked for the darts team will be pinned to the notice board.'

'A glass of vin rouge, please, Doris.'
 'Certainly , luv – red or white?'

A chap left the pub and was staggering along a river bank when he saw a man drowning. He jumped in and pulled him out.

At three in the morning, a policeman knocked at his door. 'Did you rescue a man from the river last night?'

'As a matter of fact, I did.'

'Well, I'm sorry to tell you he's hanged himself from a tree.'

'Is that so? And I just put him there to dry.'

A man in a crowded pub pushes his way to the front and shouts: 'I've a bad attack of yaws!'

'What's yaws?' asks the bar tender.

'A double Scotch on the rocks, thanks.'

Pub graffiti: DON'T TAKE THE PISS OUT OF GUINNESS – IT NEEDS ALL THE FLAVOUR IT CAN GET.

Three drunks left the pub and took a taxi to the railway station, arriving just as the train was about to leave.

A helpful porter managed to get two of them aboard and apologized to the one left behind.

'I wish I could have got you on that train, too,' he remarked.

'My pals will be a bit sore, too,' said the drunk. 'They were here to see me off.'

'What made you have your ears pierced, Willie?'

'I didn't intend to, but there was a bad darts player in here last week.'

Overheard in a bar: 'Did you sell any of your paintings at the art show?'

'No, but I felt quite encouraged – someone stole one.'

Two drunks left a pub in Piccadilly Circus. Suddenly, one disappeared down the Underground without a word.

Next night, they met again, and the first drunk asked his mate where he'd been.

'Well,' explained the other, 'I went down to see this mate who lives in the basement flat ... and you really ought to see his train set!'

18

How about the boozer who thought he'd been given counterfeit money in his change because two of the 10p pieces had the same date?

PubTalkPubTalkPubTalkPubTalkPubTalk

'I used to have a split personality, but we're both OK now.'

'Mean? She charges for 999 calls and irons Kleenex.'

'How's your wife?'
  'Compared to what?'

'I can only tell you this once, Muriel – I promised not to repeat it!'

'Our marriage is based on trust and understanding. She doesn't trust me and I don't understand her.'

'The doctor told me I'd have to limit my drinking to one a day. I'm up to 10 March, 1998.'

'Afraid I can't make the darts match tonight, Harry.'
  'Why not?'
  'I promised to take thingy out for our silver wedding anniversary.'

'Funny how my wife can spot blonde hairs and miss garage doors.'

Two cows went to an all-night party with a couple of Aberdeen Angus. They had a hell of a hangunder next morning.

A man who lived next door to a pub had a favourite tabby cat, which was run over and killed.

A year later, the publican was doing his accounts around midnight, when the ghost of this cat appeared, holding half its tail in its paw.

'Can you please help?' asked the ghost. 'You see, my old master has moved. This bit of tail I keep carrying around was cut off in an accident. Will you mend it for me?'

The publican put his pen down. 'I'm sorry,' he said, 'it just can't be done,'

'Why not?' asked the cat.

'Well, you see, I'm not allowed to retail spirits after half-past ten.'

This bar was doing really bad business. Not a soul in the place. I went in and ordered a double Scotch and the landlord said: 'Have it on me, pal, and let the New Year in.'

Is a tied pub a trussed house?

Sign outside Irish pub: LAST PUB TILL THE NEXT ONE.

Then there was the driver who always drank heavy so the police wouldn't lift him.

A chap staggered home from the pub early one morning and found this note from his missus:

'The day before yesterday you came home yesterday morning. Yesterday you came home this morning. So if today you come home tomorrow morning, you will find that I left you yesterday.'

This Aberdonian went into a pub in Union Street and ordered a pint of beer. As the barman handed it over, he asked: 'Do you think you could be getting a nip of whisky in that?'

'Certainly, sir,' said the barman.

'In that case ... perhaps you'd just top it up with beer?'

Pub graffiti: DON'T DRINK AND DRIVE – YOU'LL ONLY SPILL IT.

Jimmy came home from the pub and thought he'd pay his wife a compliment. 'You know, darling, drink makes you look stunningly beautiful and seductive.'

'But I haven't been drinking.'

'No, but I have.'

Barman to bleary drinker: 'How would you like your aspirin – shaken or stirred?'

McDougall was dying. He called his closest friend, McIver. 'Listen,' he said, 'we've been drinking in the same pub for forty years. After I'm gone, promise me that, each time you have a drink, you'll have one for me.'

'Ah promise,' said McIver, and McDougall died happy.

From then on, every time McIver went into the pub and ordered a drink, he had one for his mate, too.

One night, he went in and ordered only one whisky. 'What's up?' asked the barman, 'have you forgotten your friend's dying wish?'

'Not at all,' replied McIver. 'That Scotch is for McDougall. I'm on the wagon.'

Man to pal in pub: 'I'd invite you home to dinner, but you've never done me any harm.'

Sign in Irish pub: NO SMOKING, GUIDE DOGS EXCEPTED.

A man in a pub complained to a dog-owning customer: 'I was just slipping out to get a paper and your dog went for me.'

'That's funny,' said the punter, 'he won't go for me.'

In a pub loo: IF YOU FEEL STRONGLY ABOUT TOILET GRAFFITI – SIGN A PARTITION.

Docherty watched a punter in a Putney pub ask for a double whisky and a raw egg. He saw him drop the egg in the whisky, stir it round, and drink the concoction down in one gulp.

'What's the idea?' asked Docherty.

'First of all, it's none of your business,' came the reply. 'Secondly, I happen to like it. And, thirdly, it puts lead in my pencil.'

When Docherty got home, he tried the same mixture. But, after one sip, he poured it down the sink.

'What's going on?' asked O'Mally, his roommate.

'First of all, it's none of your business,' replied Docherty. 'Secondly, I don't like it. And, thirdly, I use a Biro.'

An Englishman, an Irishman and a Scotsman went to a party. The Englishman took six bottles of Watney's, the Irishman took six bottles of Guinness, and the Scotsman took six of his pals.

Drunk to barman: 'Isn't it amazing? Every time I breath in and out, somebody dies somewhere in the world.'

Barman: 'Have you ever tried using a mouthwash?'

Notice in pub: WHY RISK A HANGOVER? STAY DRUNK!

'Tell me the truth, doctor,' pleaded Syd. 'Don't frighten me with long words. Just tell me what's wrong in plain, straightforward English.'

'Very well,' said the doctor frankly. 'You drink too much.'

'Thanks doc,' replied Syd. 'Now ... would you tell me in long, complicated words, so I can go home and tell the wife?'

Two women in pub. 'I hear your hubby's in hospital, Mary?'

'That's right – it's his knee, you know.'

'What about it?'
'I found his secretary on it.'

This bar tender served a very weak whisky and soda. 'Tell me,' asked a customer, 'which did you put in first – the whisky or the soda?'

'The whisky, sir,' said the bar tender.

'Ah, that explains it. No doubt I'll come to it in good time.'

Then there was the guest at a Limerick hotel who rang the bar to order a drink. The barman rang back to ask the room number.

Pub graffiti: ALL THIS BEER DRINKING WILL BE THE URINATION OF ME.

A fellow was having a drink in the pub when he noticed a man wearing a wellington boot on his head.

'Excuse me,' he said at last, 'I couldn't help but notice you're wearing a welly on your head. Are you doing it for a wager?'

'Not at all,' came the reply. 'It's perfectly simple. You see. I always wear a welly on my head on Tuesdays.'

'But today happens to be Thursday.'

'Is it really? Thanks for mentioning it. I

must look bloody ridiculous!'

Pub graffiti: THE PRINCE OF ALES WAS HERE.

Two men in pub. 'Every night my wife covers her face in melon and mango yoghurt.'
    'Does it help?'
    'A bit – but I can still tell it's her.'

Pub sign: 'Don't drink if you're driving. There's no cure for the mourning after.'

'Tell me,' said the psychiatrist to the gloomy Aberdonian, 'when did you first start to enjoy standing a round?'

PubTalkPubTalkPubTalkPubTalkPubTalk

'Why do you smoke a hundred fags a day, Bert?'
    'Well, coughing is the only exercise I get.'

'Remember I bet a fiver I'd beat my drink problem?'
    'Yes.'

26

'Well, I did. Now I've got a gambling problem.'

'I thought you said you joined a fife band?'
    'So I did – but they ran out of bananas.'

'Hi, Jimmy. Haven't seen you for six months. What have you been doing?'
    'Six months.'

'When did you get the feeling your marriage was over, Rita?'
    'When he stopped lifting his visor to kiss me goodbye.'

'I hear AC Milan are after Charlie Nicholas.'
    'Yes – and Fray Bentos are after the rest of the team.'

'What's that on your cheek?'
    'A birthmark.'
    'Have you had it long?'

Standing at the bar, a chap noticed an attractive-looking girl sitting nearby.
    'Who's the bird?' he asked the barman.
    'Keep away from her,' warned the barman, 'she's a Lesbian.'
    'Really?' said the fellow and strolled over anyway.
    'Tell me, miss,' he asked pleasantly, 'which part of Libya are you from?'

After working in the Middle East, Eddie went back gratefully to his local one Saturday night.

'You know,' he said nostalgically to the barmaid, 'it's all of ten months since I've been in here.'

'Look,' she replied, 'this is my first night – I'm serving as fast as I can.'

There are two kinds of Irishmen – drunk and not yet.

A man was lamenting in the pub that his doctor had ordered him to give up half his sex life.

'Which half?' asked his mate. 'Talking about it or thinking about it?'

Then there was the boozer who read so much about the evils of drinking that he gave up reading.

Three Irishmen, on their first visit to England, were advised by a priest not to drink in any pub other than a Bass house. 'We promise, Father,' they said.

In the first pub they came to, they asked: 'Is this a Bass house?'

'No,' came the reply, 'it's a Charrington.'

In the next, they asked again. 'Sorry,' came the reply, 'this is a Watney.'

Finally, in the third, they asked again. 'Yes, they were assured, 'this is a Bass house.'

'In that case,' said one, 'could we have three pints of Guinness?'

'Dip my headlights?' said the tipsy driver to the policeman. '*What in?*'

This drunk was crawling about the pavement under a lamppost. 'What are you looking for, sir?' asked a curious policeman.

'My car keys,' came the reply.

'Where did you lose them?'

'Over there, where my car is parked.'

'But why are you looking here?'

'Well, you see, officer, the light is much better here.'

NOTICE IN BAR

If angry wives or girl friends call, our answering charges are:
- 'He's just left' – 25p.
- 'He's on his way' – 40p.
- 'He's not here' – £1.
- 'WHO did you say?' – £2.50.

Sign in pub: 'One for the road could be the pint of no return.'

These three tortoises in a pub ran out of cigarettes. One agreed to go to the machine round the corner and get some.

After three hours, the other two tortoises were getting a bit restless. 'What do you suppose is keeping him?' they wondered.

Just then, the pub door opened and the third tortoise said: 'If you're going to start talking about me behind my back, I won't go at all.'

When the new barman in the pub was asked if he had any half Coronas, he replied: 'Orange or plain lemonade, sir?'

Then there was the punter who thought Slim Panatellas was a country and western singer.

Bob paid £500 for a talking dog, and took it into the pub to show his pals. 'Looks at this,' he said, 'a dog that talks. How about that?'

'Come off it,' said one. 'I'll offer you a fiver at ten to one it doesn't say a word.'

'You're on,' said Bob. 'Now then, Rover, *talk*?' He wheedled, threatened, cajoled, but the dog refused to say a word. A furious Bob paid up and stalked out.

Outside the pub, he turned on the dog. 'Why didn't you say something, you stupid animal?' he stormed.

'Not so much of the stupid,' said the dog. 'Think of the odds you'll get next time!'

This chap was sitting in a bar drinking double brandies. Finally, he asked for a single brandy, which he downed in one.

'That's your lot, sir,' said the barman. 'I think you'd better leave.'

'I suppose you're right,' said the fellow. 'You know, it's a funny thing — the less I drink, the drunker I get.'

A fellow was enjoying a bar lunch, when an attractive blonde came in and ordered a cottage cheese sandwich.

'Are you on a low calorie diet?' asked the chap pleasantly.

'No,' came the reply, 'a low salary diet.'

An optimist says the bottle of Scotch is half full. A pessimist says it's half empty.

A drunk stopped a wealthy man in the street and asked for a handout.

'I'm sorry, my man,' came the reply, 'but I make it a rule never to hand out money in the street.'

'So what should I do – open an office?'

Pub graffiti: OLIVER REED IS IN THE RECORD BOOK OF GUINNESS.

How about the Cardiff pub that has an entrance fee of 2p? It's to keep out the riff-raff.

Two newly-wed girls in the pub lounge were discussing the sexual prowess of their respective hubbies. One complained hers wasn't too good.

'Look,' said the other, 'get him to take some rhino-horn pills. You'll be amazed at the difference.'

A couple of months later, the two got together again. 'How did you get on with the rhino-horn pills?' asked the first.

'Fantastic,' replied the other happily. 'There's just one snag. Every time he sees a Land Rover, he tries to charge it.'

Pub graffiti: TRY CIDER WITH ROSÉ.

This flea spent the evening in the pub. At closing time, he hopped out, leapt in the air and fell flat on his face. 'Dammit,' he said, 'someone's moved my dog!'

A feller dashes into the pub. 'Quick,' he shouts, 'give me a pint of bitter before the row starts.'

The barman pulls him a pint, which he knocks back in one go. 'Give us another pint,' he demands, 'before the row starts.'

So the barman gives him another, and he finishes that. 'Another pint, please,' he asks, 'before the row starts.'

'Wait a minute,' said the barman, 'what's all this about a row starting?'

'Well, it's like this,' says the chap, 'I've no money.'

'Hey, Willie, do you believe in drinking whisky to cure a cold?'

'Only as a first resort, Jock.'

A police car stopped at a lay-by, where a driver was knocking back stout and throwing the bottles out of the window.

'What's the big idea?' asked the sergeant.

'Well, you see,' explained the driver, 'I'm on the works outing.'

'Works outing? But where are all the

others?'

'What others? I'm self-employed!'

Pub graffiti: I NEVER DO ANYTHING BY HALVES – MINE'S A PINT.

Five animals were having a cocktail party when the barman asked for payment.

The skunk said: 'I've only one cent.'

The duck said: 'I've only one bill and I'm not going to break into that.'

The deer said: 'I had a buck on me earlier, but it will be some time before I get a little dough.'

The cow said: 'Let the udders pay.'

And the giraffe said resignedly: 'Well, I guess the highballs are on me.'

Girl to girl in pub: 'If you're so fed up with your marriage, why don't you leave him?'

'I would – if I could find a way of doing it without making him happy.'

'Sorry I'm late, darling, but I was competing in a beer-drinking contest in the pub.'

'Oh, really? And who came second?'

This motorist was weaving about the road when a police car drew up. 'Would you mind blowing this up?' asked the sergeant, handing him a balloon.

'No problem,' said the drunk. 'Who's in goal?'

'Did you hear Des O'Connor's last record, Fred?'

'I hope so.'

PubTalkPubTalkPubTalkPubTalkPubT2alk

'Want to buy a watch, Derek?'

'Sure – let's see it.'

'Sssh – the fellow next to you is wearing it!'

'What's this about you having your living-room piled with crates of Guinness?'

'Well, if that's not living, I don't know what is.'

'I really ought to have the curry, but I just don't have the guts.'

'What does Charlie do for a living?'

'He's a joiner. Whenever he sees someone going into a pub, he joins them.'

'Yes, our holiday had everything ... quiet pubs for me, sunny beaches for the wife, sharks for the mother-in-law ... '

'I thought you were an atheist?'
'So I was, but I gave it up – no holidays.'

'Why do you call your wife Cap'n Morgan?'
'Because she's got a sunken chest.'

'Why do you think so many people take an instant dislike to me?'
'Saves time.'

A man walked into this pub with his dog. 'A pint of lager,' he asked the barman. 'And I'll have a half,' said the dog.

The barman was astonished. 'That's some dog,' he said. 'Do you think he'd fetch me a newspaper if I gave him some money?'

'Of course I would,' said the dog, finishing his drink, and trotted off.

After about two hours, the dog staggered back on his knees. 'Where the hell have YOU been?' asked the irate owner.

'Well,' replied the dog, 'I met this bitch down the lane, and one thing led to another ... '

'You've never done THAT before,' remonstrated the owner.

'I've never had the money before,' replied the dog.

I wouldn't say McPherson was drunk, but, two weeks after he died, his liver won a breakdancing contest.

Chap in pub: 'What's up, Gerry, you seem depressed.'

'Not without reason,' replied Gerry. 'My wife reversed the car out of the garage this morning.'

'So?'

'I reversed it INTO the garage last night!'

How about the drinker who asked for a couple of cherries in his bitter? The doctor had told him to eat more fruit.

A drunk was staggering down the road, when he saw a motorist, bonnet up, looking into his engine.

'What's the matter, Jimmy?' asked the drunk.

'Piston broke,' came the reply.

'Me, too,' said the drunk, lurching off.

How about the go-go dancer in the pub who didn't get paid? She went-went.

'Please don't talk to me,' said the minister to the drunk. 'You're under the influence.'

'You're no worse than me,' came the reply. 'At least my collar's on the right way round.'

These two fellers were ordering pub grub. 'And we'll have two glasses of white wine,' said one. 'Make sure I get a clean glass. The one you gave me last week was filthy.'

The waiter brought the food and the wine. 'Here we are, then,' he said. 'Now ... which of you wanted the clean glass?'

Three ex-Army men met in a pub. The Englishman stood a round, the Irishman stood a round, and the Scotsman stood 6 ft 2 in.

Sign in bar: 'If you suddenly notice our colour TV – don't drive. It's black and white.'

A chap stood at the end of the bar, looking thoroughly miserable. 'What's up, chum?' asked one of the regulars.

'I'm lonely,' complained the man.

'Never mind,' said the regular. 'It's not the end of the world. Here – let me buy you a drink.'

'Thanks,' said the man, 'I'll have a triple vodka.'

'Blimey,' said the regular, 'no wonder you're lonely!'

This police car stopped a Cortina loaded with Scots returning from a soccer international at

Wembley.

'Is this car licenced?' asked the sergeant.

'Sure is, serge,' the driver replied happily. 'Like a pint of heavy?'

Hubby came home drunk again. 'I'm fed up,' shouted his wife. 'Why do you always come home three parts sloshed?'

'I keep running out of money,' he explained.

How about the chap who suffers from alcoholic constipation? He can't pass a pub.

Ist drunk: 'Is that the sun or the moon up there?'

2nd drunk: 'Dunno ... I don't live round here.'

You can always tell a stranger in a Glasgow pub. He puts his drink down.

Two Aberdonians bumped into each other after forty years and went into the nearest pub to celebrate.

'It'll be magic to have a pint together after a' these years,' said one.

'Aye, it will,' said the other, 'but, dinna forget — it's your round!'

A drunk asked a passer-by the way to Alcoholics Anonymous. 'Do you wish to join?' asked the passer-by.

'No,' came the reply, 'to resign.'

Then there was the barmaid who had two improper suggestions made to her one night. She was quite upset about it. Normally she has ten or twelve.

This fellow in the bar asked the chap drinking next to him what he did for a living. 'I work for a carnival,' came the reply. 'I'm a human cannonball.'

'I bet that takes a lot of courage.'

'Not half. That's why I'm here now. I have to get loaded first.'

A Scottish hotel applied for a drinking licence, but it was refused 'because the roads in the vicinity are unsuitable for drunken driving.'

This chap walked into the bar, ordered two pints of lager, put one on the floor and drank the other. Then he did the same thing again.

The barman was flummoxed ... till he saw a man, four inches high, supping happily on the floor.

'Who on earth's that?' he asked in amazement.

'That's my mate, Jimmy,' came the reply. 'We served together in the Army all over the world ... from Aden to Alaska, Vietnam to Hong Kong, Africa to — hey, Jimmy, where was it you called that witchdoctor a gormless yobbo ... ?'

A man was drinking in a pub, minding his own business. When he went outside, he found someone had painted his car bright green.

In a fury, he rushed back in and demanded to know the culprit. Whereupon a seven-foot Mr Universe stood up and admitted it was him. 'And what are you going to do about it?' he added.

'Not a lot,' said the man. 'I just thought you'd like to know the first coat's dry.'

Bert got home from the pub one night the worse for wear, and headed straight for the bathroom.

'Is that bottle of green stuff shampoo?' he shouted.

'No,' said his wife, 'it's superglue.'

'No wonder I couldn't get my hat off in the pub.'

Pub graffiti: LOCKJAW MEANS NEVER HAVING TO SAY YOU'RE SORRY.

How about the Chelsea fans who beat the ban on booze by carrying in the stuff internally?

Murphy got into a pub fight with a much bigger man, and was left lying flat out on the floor.

'Have you had enough now?' asked the big man.

'I don't know,' replied Murphy. 'This is my first fight.'

This commercial traveller went into a country pub and started chatting with the locals. After a while, the talk turned to politics.

'I can't stand Maggie Thatcher,' said the traveller. 'Her face looks like a sheep's head.'

Half an hour later, he came round in the car park, bruised and beaten up.

'What was that for?' he asked in a daze. 'I didn't know anyone felt so strongly for Mrs Thatcher. Is this Tory territory, or what?'

'No,' came the stern reply. '*Sheep* territory!'

Sign in pub: 'If you like home cooking, stay home.'

Three racehorses were sitting in a pub, chatting about racing.

'Funny thing,' said the first, 'I was racing at Newmarket, not doing well, when I suddenly got this sharp pain in my rump, shot through the field, and won by a head.'

'Isn't that strange?' put in the second horse. 'A similar thing happened to me at Goodwood.'

'Extraordinary,' remarked the third. 'I had exactly the same experience at Sandown.'

Just then, a greyhound, sipping brandy, went over to the horses' table and said: 'Excuse me, but I happened to overhear. You'll never believe this, but exactly the same thing happened to me at the White City.'

The racehorses looked at each other. 'Good heavens,' said one, 'isn't that amazing — *a talking dog*!'

'What makes you think Tommy's had enough?'

'He's just walked into that grandfather clock and tried to make a phone call.'

A couple were driving home after a party. Said the wife: 'Well, you certainly made a fool of yourself tonight. I just hope nobody realized you were sober.'

Pub graffiti: WHEN GOD CREATED MAN, SHE WAS ONLY JOKING.

The landlord of a pub watched quietly as the barman put 50p in his pocket out of every pound he took from a customer.

Then he spotted the barman putting an entire £1 note into his own wallet.

'What do you think you're doing?' asked the landlord. 'I thought we were partners!'

Pal in pub: 'Did you give your wife that lecture on economy like I told you?'

'I certainly did.'

'Any result?'

'Yes – I've to give up smoking.'

Scrawled in pub loo: 'People who drink too much should be treated by a doctor.' Underneath someone wrote: 'People who drink too much don't mind who treats them.'

This dolly bird rushes into a pub and demands a Campari and soda.

'How old are you, miss?' asks the barman.

'Sixteen,' replies the girl.

'Then you've had it,' says the barman.

'I know,' pants the girl, 'that's what's made me so thirsty.'

PubTalkPubTalkPubTalkPubTalkPubTalk

'Today's the wife's birthday.'

  'What are you getting for her?'

  'What are you offering?'

'Won't your wife hit the ceiling tonight when you walk in at this hour?'

  'Probably. She's a lousy shot.'

'Hey, Jimmy, can you smell my breath?'

  'Naw ... the beer hides it.'

'What's the soup du jour, barman?'

  'It's off – we ran out of it yesterday.'

'I just fell down the stairs with fifteen pints of Guinness.'

  'Did you spill any?'

  'No, I kept my mouth closed.'

'I thought you said you get drunk after one whisky?'

  'Aye – usually the seventeenth.'

The odd-looking dog in the pub was a big talking point. Eventually, one of the regulars said to the owner: 'That's a stupid-looking dog. Can it fight?'

'Sure,' said the owner.

'Well,' said the man, 'I'll bet you £20 my alsatian can beat your dog.'

The owner accepted the bet, and the two dogs were led in to fight. In just twenty-two seconds, the alsatian lay dead on the floor.

The loser paid over the money. 'Your dog can certainly fight,' he admitted, 'but I still think it's a funny-looking animal.'

'It looked even funnier,' said the owner, 'before I shaved its mane off.'

Two Spurs supporters went to Rome for a European Cup game – this is an old joke – and were discussing where to meet the next day.

'I know,' said one brightly, 'let's meet at the Vatican.'

'Good idea,' said the other, 'the lounge or the saloon?'

Harvey Smith had five clear rounds at Hickstead the other day, and was then asked to leave by the landlord.

How about the member of the Campaign For Real Ale, who was drinking one night in a topless bar? He said the beer was all right, but complained that the waitress was flat.

A stranger went into the pub. 'Good evening, sir,' said the landlord. 'I haven't seen you here before. Would you like a drink?'

'Yes, please,' came the reply. 'I'll have a large malt whisky.'

Said the landlord: 'That will be £1.70, please.'

'Oh, no,' said the stranger. 'I distinctly remember you *inviting* me to have a drink. I thought it was very kind of you.'

The landlord turned to a regular customer, a solicitor, and asked for support.

But the solicitor confirmed that the landlord had made a definite offer, which the man had accepted, so no money should change hands.

The landlord was furious, turned the man out of the pub, and told him never to come back.

Ten minutes later, the man reappeared. 'I thought I told you never to return,' said the landlord.

'I've never been here before in my life,' said the man.

'Then you must have a double,' said the landlord.

'Thanks very much,' came the reply, 'and one for our solicitor friend while you're at it.'

Heard about the publican who was run over by his own lorry? It's the first time the drinks have been on him.

This kangaroo hops into a pub and orders a pint of Watney's. He puts a fiver on the bar and the barman give him £1 change. The kangaroo drinks up, puts the pounds in his pouch and starts to leave.

'Excuse me for mentioning it,' says the barman, 'but we don't get many kangaroos in here.'

'I'm not surprised,' remarks the kangaroo, 'with beer at £4 a pint.'

Wife: 'Another night spent boozing in the pub. What's the excuse this time?'

Hubby: 'Well, there I was, a drink in my hands, in front of a blazing fire. It was very difficult to leave.'

'You could always have got up and walked out.'

'What ... with all those firemen in the way?'

Man in pub: 'I'm a man of simple tastes. Give me a bottle of whisky, a tin of biscuits and a dog and I'm perfectly happy.'

'Why the dog?' asked his pal.

'Well, *someone's* got to eat the biscuits!'

Pub sign: 'Have you tried our home-made pies? You'll never get better.'

Fred staggered home very late and very drunk. All the way from the pub, he kept trying to think of a way of appearing sober in front of his wife.

At last, he decided to be absorbed in a book when he got home.

His wife came storming downstairs. 'And what do you think *you're* up to?' she asked.

'Nothing, dear, just reading,' came the reply.

'Well, when you've come to the end of the chapter, close the suitcase and come to bed!'

Car sticker: BAR TENDERS DO IT ON THE ROCKS.

A docker came running down the road and was stopped by a policeman. 'Why exactly are you running?' he asked.

'I'm having a race with this bloke for a pint of bitter,' said the docker ... so the policeman let him go.

Then another chap dashes up, puffing and panting. 'Why on earth did you let him go?' he asked the policeman.

'He said he was having a race for a pint of bitter.'

'I know – I'm the landlord. He left without paying for it!'

'Why did you move next door to the brewery, Bert?'
  'Well, the air is more intoxicating.'

PubTalkPubTalkPubTalkPubTalkPubTalk

'A Martini, please.'
  'A dry one, sir?'
  'Good heavens, no – I'm far too thirsty.'

'What was it like having all your teeth out?'
  'Phew – never again.'

'I was clueless when I got married, Marlene. I couldn't even get him to boil an egg.'

'The trouble with you, Arthur, is you've no sense of humour.'
  'I don't think that's very funny.'

'Do you always drink your whisky neat?'
  'No – sometimes I let my shirt hang out.'

'The wife took her cookery exam last week.'
  'How did she get on?'
  'She got full marks for defrosting.'

This chap joined a posh golf club. On his first day, he went into the bar and asked for a double whisky. When he came to pay, the barman said: 'That's all right, sir. Drinks are on the house.'

So the fellow went to the professional's shop to buy some golf balls. He was amazed to be charged £20 each for them.

When his son came to pick him up later, he asked: 'How did it go, Dad?'

'Well, son,' replied the father, 'I'll tell you one thing – in this club they don't catch you by the drinks!'

'Charlie – lend us a fiver till pay day to buy a round.'

'OK – but when's pay day?'

'How should I know? You're the one who's working.'

Two men went into a pub serving pub lunches and took out packets of sandwiches.

'Hey,' said the barman, 'you can't eat your own sandwiches in here.'

So they swapped.

'Fred, if you had to give up wine or women, which would you choose?'

'That would rather depend on the vintage of each.'

This feller walks into a pub and asks the barman for a pint of beer and two pickled onions. He puts the onions behind his ears, drinks the beer and walks out. This happens six nights in a row.

On the seventh night, the barman says: 'I'm sorry, sir, we're clean out of pickled onions. But I can offer you gherkins.'

'That'll do,' says the man. He puts a gherkin behind each ear, drinks the beer, and is about to leave, when the barman stops him.

'Excuse me, sir,' he says. 'Every day you've come in here, ordered a pint and two pickled onions, put them behind your ears, drunk your pint and walked out. Tonight you've put two *gherkins* behind your ears. Tell me – why on earth do you do it?'

'Well,' said the man, 'you haven't any pickled onions, have you?'

Wife to hubby: 'No, I don't mind if you go down to the pub. Now ask me if I'll let you come back in.'

A heavy drinker went to the doctor for a check-up. 'It's quite clear to me,' said the doctor, 'that alcohol is entirely responsible for your poor physical shape.'

'Thank God for that, doc – the wife keeps insisting it's my fault.'

Pub notice: 'All our sausages made with the best conservatives.'

Two men met in a bar. 'I'm a traveller and I've just landed a big order,' said one. 'I'm trying to think of a suitable gift to take my wife.'

'I know the perfect present,' said the other. 'Buy her a dress. No matter how many dresses she has, she'll always enjoy another one. Believe me, nothing makes a woman happier than something new to wear.'

'I never thought of that,' said the traveller. 'Tell me, are you by any chance a psychologist?'

'No,' said the other, 'I'm a dress manufacturer.'

Willie said to Archie in the pub: 'I've a funny feeling my wife is up to something. Whenever I go home for lunch, she looks a bit flustered and dishevelled.'

'What time do you go home for lunch?' asked Archie.

'About one o'clock.'

'Tell you what – why don't you go home at 12.30 tomorrow?'

Willie agreed and went home early next lunchtime. When the two met again in the bar, Archie asked what had happened.

'I went upstairs and found her in bed with another man,' said Willie.

'Then what did you do?'

'I went downstairs and made some lunch for myself.'

'What about the other man?'

'Let him make his own bloody lunch!'

Doctor: 'Now, remember, Patrick, just add one teaspoonful of medicine to your pint of Guinness.'

Patrick: 'Er ... would that be heaped or level, doctor?'

PubTalkPubTalkPubTalkPubTalkPubTalk

'Tony, you drive – you're far too drunk to sing.'

'This Pat Pending sure comes up with a lot of good gadgets.'

'Why do you drink, Charlie?'

'Booze killed my mother and booze killed my father. I'm drinking for revenge.'

'At my funeral, I want you to pour a bottle of Haig's over my grave, Jimmy.'

'I'll be glad to, Hector. You don't mind if it passes through my kidneys first?'

'I thought you said you never drink till noon?'

'It's noon in Bangkok!'

'Barman, this beer's a bit cloudy.'

'What do you want for 70p – thunder and lightning?'

Sign in Aberdeen pub: 'Free drink for pensioners, if accompanied by parents.'

A man was driving down a country road in heavy rain, when he spotted a chap sloshing along, looking thoroughly miserable. So he stopped and offered him a lift, which was gratefully accepted.

'Where are you going in this awful weather?' asked the driver.

'Just three miles down the road to the pub,' came the reply. 'I always have a nip of whisky every day.'

'Have you thought of keeping a bottle in the house for weather like this?'

'Many a time ... but, at my house, whisky don't keep.'

'Ish this Wembley?' asked the tipsy football fan.

'No, it's Thursday.'

'So am I – le'sh have a drink.'

How about the punter who walks into a pub and says: 'Give us a crocodile sandwich and make it snappy.'

Wife to hubby: 'As a matter of fact, I DO feel like coming with you to a stuffy old pub!'

Andy came home dead drunk and broke. 'What did you do with your wages?' demanded his wife.

'I bought something for the house,' came the reply.

'What did you buy for the house that cost £95?'

'Six rounds of drinks.'

Two drunks out walking got separated. Said one to a policeman: 'Excuse me, ossifer, but have you seen a feller wandering about without me?'

A fellow wandered into a pub. 'Get out,' said the barman. 'I remember you. For the past five nights you've come in here, got drunk, smashed up the furniture, assaulted the customers and threatened me with my life.'

'You've got the wrong man,' said the chap. 'I swear I've never been in this pub in my life.'

'Well, I suppose I could have been mistaken,' said the barman grudgingly. 'Let's forget it. I'll buy you a drink. What'll it be?'

'Thanks,' said the fellow. 'I'll have the usual.'

O'Toole left the pub and staggered into a wake in a Dublin house. Instead of looking into the coffin, he lifted up the lid of the piano. 'I don't know who he was,' he said, 'but, by God, he had a marvellous set of teeth!'

A fellow staggered into Alcoholics Anonymous, fell over a chair and finished in a crumpled, drunken heap on the floor.

'Oh, dear,' said the secretary, 'when you turned up sober last time, you made me so happy.'

'Well,' burped the drunk, 'today it's *my* turn to be happy!'

'Hey, barman, I ordered a pint – this glass is only three-quarters full.'

'Oh, that's a pint, all right, sir – I just packed it in very tightly.'

Notice beside a bowl of peanuts in bar: 'The drinking man's filter.'

Tough? This Liverpool pub was so tough that, as the punters came in, they were frisked for weapons. If they didn't have any – they were given one.

'How did you come to break your leg, Sandy?'

'I saw a spider on the pub ceiling and tried to step on it.'

Then there was the Aberdonian who held up a ship launching for three hours. He wouldn't let go of the bottle.

A feller in a pub says: 'I know your face.' The other feller says: 'I don't know you.'

'I've got it,' says the first. 'We were prisoners-of-war in Silesia, and escaped disguised as nuns on the back of a lorryload of lentils.'

'No, it wasn't me,' says the other.

'I know,' says the first. 'We sheltered together on Etna when it erupted, and we escaped by sliding down on cooling lava.'

'No,' says the other feller, 'it wasn't me.'

'I've got it,' says the first. 'We went shark fishing off the Great Barrier Reef, and you fell in love with a nymphomaniac pearl diver.'

'No, it definitely wasn't me,' insists the other.

A pause. Then the first feller says: 'Did you

happen to be in the pub last night?'

'Yes, as a matter of fact, I was.'

'Well, *that's* where I've seen you!'

Three men in a pub found flies in their beer. The Englishman picked the fly out with his finger. The Irishman took his out with a toothpick. And the Scotsman *wrung* his out.

Heard about the new lager for easy-going girls which refreshes the parts that anyone can reach?

PubTalkPubTalkPubTalkPubTalkPubTalk

'The wife's a kleptomaniac.'

'Is she taking anything for it?'

'Has a lemon got legs?'

'Of course not.'

'Then I've just squeezed a canary into my gin.'

'Give us a fag, Donald.'

'I thought you'd stopped smoking?'

'Well, I've reached the first stage – I've stopped buying them.'

'I hear your wife does bird impressions?'

'That's right – she watches me like a hawk.'

'Fred's taken up meditation, Myra.'
    'Well, I suppose it's better than sitting around doing nothing.'

'Do you believe in free love, Albert?'
    'Have I ever sent you an invoice?'

A feller in the pub claimed his dog could play a passable game of poker.
    'That's incredible,' said his pal.
    'Not really,' said the bloke. 'When he gets a really good hand, he wags his tail.'

You know you're getting old when you have that morning-after feeling without having had the night before.

'Excuse me, where's the nearest pub in this town?'
    'Let me see, now – it's seven miles away. Unless, of course, you go in the other direction, in which case it's only three hundred yards.'

A drunk was trying to open the door of his house early one morning, when a policeman approached and helped him in.
    The drunk insisted on giving the policeman

a guided tour. 'This is the lounge – this is the kitchen – this is the hallway – these are the stairs.'

As he opened the bedroom door, the drunk went on: 'And this is the bedroom, this is my bed, that's my wife, and the man lying next to her – *that's me*!'

How about the tipsy elephant who kept seeing little pink men?

The police car stopped a car that was doing a steady 30 mph to congratulate the driver on going so carefully.

'That's all right, officer,' put in his wife, 'he always watches it when he's had one too many.'

A shortage of Guinness in a Dublin pub didn't upset the customers. The barman served them lager with sun glasses.

'Sorry, sir,' said the barman, 'you can't pay for five pints of bitter with Luncheon Vouchers.'

'Why not?' asked the customer, 'that *is* my lunch!'

This drunk threw himself out of a ninth floor window.

As he lay on the pavement, a young woman asked: 'What happened?'

'Don't ask me,' said the drunk, 'I've only just got here myself.'

Definition of a local anaesthetic: Getting stoned in your favourite pub.

Heard about Alcoholics Anonymous Russian roulette? They pass round glasses of tomato juice ... and one of them is a Bloody Mary.

Drunk in a pub: 'Just look at that ugly old bag over there? What a face – enough to stop a clock.'

Stranger: 'She happens to be my wife.'

Drunk: 'Nice legs ... '

'Excuse me, sir,' said the down-and-out in the pub. 'Could you spare £1.60 for a double whisky?'

'Wouldn't 35p for a cup of coffee be more like it?'

'Ordinarily, yes. But, you see, today's my wedding anniversary.'

When One-Eyed Riley gets drunk, does he see single?

Drunk in public bar: 'I must be going mad. Every time I ask someone the time, I get a different answer!'

Barman: 'Tell me, if your missus is so beautiful, why do you get drunk every night?'
     Boozer: 'So I can see two of her.'

'Did you just pour beer in my lap?'
     'No, pal ... what you have there is an inside job.'

Pub sign: 'Don't drive yourself to drink. Get a chauffeur.'

An English soldier wandered into a pub in Belfast one lunchtime. Four IRA men barred his way. 'You're not coming in here,' they said.
     A scuffle followed, which ended with the IRA men lying unconscious on the floor.
     The soldier walked to the bar, bought a pint of bitter and a pie. Then he took a knife, cut an

ear off one of the IRA men, popped it in his pie, and ate it.

'Tell me,' asked the puzzled barman, 'what sort of a soldier are you?'

'Pie-and-ear Corps,' came the reply.

Charlie arrived home late from the pub, well oiled and ready for a row.

'Is that you, Charlie?' asked his wife, as he stumbled up the stairs.

'It had flaming well better be!' replied Charlie.

This chap phoned his wife from the pub to say he'd been delayed at the office. Her voice at the other end said: 'Don't come that old rubbish again. Get out of that pub this minute and come straight home. This is a recorded announcement.'

'My first husband died of love.'

'Did he now? I heard he died of drink.'

'That's right – love of drink.'

George got very drunk in the pub and ended up being thrown out by the landlord. He staggered back, this time through the saloon door, and was again tossed out by the landlord. He then crawled in through the snug door. 'Out you go,' shouted the landlord, 'and stay out!'

George rose unsteadily to his feet. 'Tell me one thing,' he asked, 'do you own ALL the flaming pubs round here?'

At a funeral in Birmingham, one of the mourners was asked who had died. 'I dunno,' came the reply, 'I'm only here for the bier.'

Two men in the bar. One was staring at the other. 'You know what?' he said finally, 'you remind me of my girl friend. If it weren't for the moustache, you could be her twin.'

'But I don't have a moustache.'

'I know, but my girl friend does.'

Pub graffiti: WHERE WILL YOU BE ON JUDGEMENT DAY? Underneath someone scrawled: 'Still waiting for the flipping bus.'

Barman on phone: 'Lady, this bar is packed with good-for-nothing layabout husbands. You'll have to give me a better description.'

'I wouldn't say he lived to drink, but every time he bends his elbow, his mouth snaps open.'

'Fred has the energy of a man twice his age.'

'I may have my faults, Mary, but being wrong isn't one of them.'

'I was living the life of Riley – then Riley came home.'

'I hate repeating gossip, Sandra – but what else can you do with it?'

'I thought you were working as a cab driver?'
  'I was – but I didn't like people talking behind my back.'

'I've had an absolutely frightful day, looking for a job for mother.'

'Why's Charlie crying in his beer?'
  'He won the pools the same day as his boss.'

A feller won £2000 at the races and went to the pub to celebrate. Returning home in the early hours, he crept into bed beside his wife and slipped the money under his pillow.
  In the morning, he put his hand under the pillow and his face went white.
  'What's the matter, dear?' asked his wife.

'You look terrible.'
    'Yes,' said the chap, 'I don't feel too grand.'

'What's in that new locket you're wearing, Maggie?'
    'It's a lock of my hubby's hair.'
    'He's still around, though, isn't he?'
    'Yes – but his hair isn't.'

Two men in a pub. 'I'm going to get a divorce,' says one. 'The wife hasn't said a word to me in six months.'
    'Think it over,' advised his pal. 'Wives like that are hard to find.'

Man to barmaid: 'Gladys – tell me I'm not just four pints of bitter and twenty fags a night to you.'

This chap went with a pal to an athletics meeting. The bar was at 7 ft 9 in. No-one could get a bloody drink!

'How did you get on at the doctor's, Charlie?'
    'He told me to take a pill every day for the rest of my life.'

'That's not so bad.'
'No? He only gave me three.'

Notice in Bermondsey bar: 'Please do not leave the bar while room is in motion.'

The wife was moaning about her hubby going out drinking night after night. So, one evening, he took her along to the local.

'What'll you have?' he asked. 'The same as you,' she replied. So he ordered two pints of bitter.

She took one mouthful and spat it out. 'I don't know how you drink this stuff,' she said. 'It tastes awful.'

'There you are,' said the husband, 'and you think I'm out enjoying myself every night!'

How about the woman who phoned the doctor to ask him to come round, as the baby had swallowed the corkscrew? Ten minutes later, she phoned back and told him not to bother, as she'd found another corkscrew.

'Can't stay long, Arthur,' said the man in the pub. 'The wife thinks I'm in the bath.'

A chap in the bar was propositioned by the attractive barmaid. Near closing time, she said to him: 'Come to my flat tonight and I'll show you a good time. I've a super place … mirrors on the walls, mirrors on the floor, mirrors on the ceiling. How about it?'

'OK,' said the chap. 'I'll be there.'

'Come after 11 pm,' she added, 'and be sure to bring a bottle.'

The feller arrived on the dot, to be met by the barmaid in a silky black negligée and smelling of Chanel No. 5.

'Come in, darling,' she murmured. 'Did you remember the bottle?'

The fellow took his cap off, dipped into his plastic carrier bag and handed the bottle over.

'What's this stuff?' she asked. 'It's pink.'

'It's always that colour,' said the chap, 'it's Windowlene.'

Two men in pub. 'This time tomorrow,' says one, 'I'll be on the plane.'

'Going to Benidorm?' asks the other.

'No – taking three inches off the door.'

This piglet goes into the pub and asks for a double whisky – and another – and another – and another. 'Aren't you drinking rather a lot for a piglet?' asks the barman.

'Oh, I don't know,' comes the reply. 'You see, I'm the little piggy who goes "wee, wee, wee" all the way home!'

Pub graffiti: GIN AND BEER IT.

PubTalkPubTalkPubTalkPubTalkPubTalk

'Have you flu, Jimmy?'
  'Naw – Ah came by bus.'

'Is it true you've haven't spoken to your missus in six weeks?'
  'That's right – I didn't want to interrupt her.'

'There's a rumour going round that you're dead.'
  'I heard that rumour myself. But, when I checked it out, I discovered it was some other guy.'

'I passed your house yesterday.'
  'Thanks.'

'Whisky and soda, sir?'
  'Yes, please – without the soda.'

'My hubby's a man of rare gifts – he hasn't given me one in years.'

'This bloke is so lazy he married a pregnant woman.'

'Posh? She waters her pot plants with Perrier water.'

70

'Hey, Joe, did you hear about Archie?'

'No – what?'

'He came home early from work last night, found his wife in bed with Victor, and shot them both.'

'Well, I suppose it might have been worse.'

'How do you mean?'

'Well, if Archie had come home early the night before, I'd be dead by now.'

This chap having a pub lunch complained about his chicken and camel stew.

'What's wrong with it?' asked the waiter.

'What's wrong with it?' echoed the chap. 'It's ninety per cent camel, that's what!'

The waiter went away to have a word with the cook. Then he came back and said: 'I've been told to tell you it's half and half – half a chicken to half a camel.'

Then there was the trader who did a roaring business selling square-bottomed glasses to pubs. His sales patter went: 'They don't leave rings on bars or tables.'

'Barman – two Martinis, one with an olive and one without.'

'Certainly, sir – which one?'

A cruiser registered at a Cheshire club is named Cirrhosis of the River.

This drunk was sitting at the bar, sobbing his heart out.

'What's the matter?' asked the sympathetic barman.

'I've done a terrible thing,' confessed the drunk. 'Last night, I sold my wife for a bottle of White Horse.'

'I quite understand,' said the barman, 'and now you wish you had her back?'

'That's right,' said the drunk, 'I'm thirsty again.'

Peter arrived home late from the pub, drunk as usual. But, this time, his wife tried a new technique. The table was laid with an exotic meal, the room lit by candles, and soft music played.

'Hello, dearest,' she purred in her flimsy negligée. 'I've a lovely bottle of wine to go with the food. And afterwards we can retire to bed.'

'Why not?' said Peter. 'But if the wife ever finds out, she'll kill me.'

'Your glass is empty, Muldoon. Will you be havin' another?'

'Sure what would I want with two empty glasses?'

'Hey, darling, what happened to that skinny blonde your old man used to be married to?'

'I dyed my hair.'

This chap went into a pub and had a ploughman's lunch. The ploughman was furious.

'Hey, barman, this bowl of soup you brought – the bowl is filthy.'

'No, sir, the bowl is clean – it's the soup that's dirty.'

Man in bar: 'Give us a gin, Ivor.' The barman handed one over, whereupon the chap dropped an Oxo cube in it.

'What do you call that?' asked the barman.

'Oxogin,' the man replied.

Six skinheads in a pub. They walk up to this table where a meek and mild fellow is starting a meal. Between them, they eat all his dinner, mop up the plate with his bread, finish off his tea, and hit him over the head with the empty cup. The chap just gets up and walks out.

'Not much of a man, was he?' says one of the skinheads to the barman.

'He's not much of a driver, either,' remarks

the barman. 'He's just jumped in his lorry and driven over six motorbikes in the car park.'

How about the football manager who told his team to go right out and enjoy themselves? They did – and went straight to the nearest bar.

Two storks were chatting in the Stork Club.
   'Any business today?'
   'No – but I put the wind up a couple of secretaries.'

Three old men in the pub were discussing how they would like to die.
   'I'd like to die after planting a flag on the top of Everest,' said one.
   Said the second: 'I'd like to die after taking a wicket with the last ball of a Test match, and so winning the Ashes for England.'
   And the third said: 'I'd like to die in bed – shot by a jealous husband.'

Then there was the chap who walked into a pub carrying a parking meter, so he'd remember where he parked his car.

'Is it true your hubby's a hard drinker?'

'No – he finds it the easiest thing in the world.'

How about the feller who gave up the fiddle and learnt to play the piano? His beer kept sliding off the fiddle.

A drunk staggered home to be met in the hall by his wife. 'Would you like your kiss neat?' he asked, 'or shall I take a swig of lemonade first?'

Pub graffiti: SUPPORT FULHAM – WHY SUFFER ALONE?

A driver, returning from a wedding with his wife and young son, was stopped by the police and breathalysed. The test showed he had been drinking. 'I'm afraid you'll have to come down to the station,' said the officer.

'Wait a minute,' said the driver, 'I haven't had a drink all day. Try the breathalyser on my ten-year-old son and see what happens.'

So the officer gave the boy the breathalyser, and, sure enough, it indicated that the *boy* had been drinking.

'It certainly looks as if the apparatus is

faulty,' admitted the officer. 'You're free to go on your way.'

The driver drove off, remarking to his wife: 'I told you it was a good idea to give the boy a double Scotch before we left!'

An Irishman walks into the pub with a big door under his arm. 'What's the idea of the door?' asked the barman.

'Well,' explained the man, 'it's a safety precaution. Last night I lost the key.'

'And what happens if you lose the door?'

'That's all right — I've left the window open.'

'Barman, whisky and ice, please.'

'Sorry, sir, no ice.'

'Then I'll have it with water.'

'I'm afraid the water's frozen.'

Car sticker: DRIVER IS SUFFERING FROM BOTTLE FATIGUE.

This feller entered a crowded bar. 'Drinks all round,' he told the barman, 'and have one yourself.'

'Thanks very much,' said the barman. 'That'll be £22.50.'

'I haven't any money,' said the chap. At that, the barman leapt over the bar, gave the man a thrashing and bundled him out.

A few weeks passed. The man returned and again ordered drinks all round.

'Does that include me?' asked the barman.

'Not likely,' replied the man. 'Give you a drink and you go raving mad!'

A man staggered out of a pub one night at closing time, fumbled with his car keys, got into the driving seat, and drove off erratically, closely followed by a couple of police cars.

Three miles down the road, the driver was signalled to pull in. 'Now, then, sir,' said one of the coppers, 'I have reason to believe you're drunk in charge of this vehicle.'

'Nonsense,' replied the driver. 'I'm perfectly sober.'

'Very well, sir,' said the law, 'I'll have to breathalyse you.' Which they did ... and found it registered negative.

'I don't understand this,' said the policeman, scratching his head.

'It's perfectly simple, officer,' said the driver. 'You see, I'm a professional decoy!'

Pub graffiti: MAKE YOUR MP WORK – DON'T RE-ELECT HIM.

Harold was out in the pub most of the night. He crept into the bedroom as dawn was breaking and started to undress.

Just then, his wife woke up. 'Harold,' she cried, 'where's your underwear?'

'My God,' cried Harold. 'I've been robbed!'

The landlord of the pub was wakened by the phone at 3 am. 'What time do you open?' asked the caller. 'Half past ten,' snapped the landlord, and slammed the phone down.

This went on for four more times, till the landlord protested: 'Look, I'm trying to get some sleep. Can't you wait to get in?'

'I'm not trying to get in,' said the caller. 'I'm trying to get out!'

Man in pub: 'Hey, Jimmy, I wanna tell you somethin' — you're a typical, hen-pecked, bloody husband.'

Jimmy: 'You wouldnae dare say that if ma' wife wiz here.'

Then there was the feller slung out of a pub because he asked for a pint of Titbread's Wankard.

Car sticker: THIS CAR'S TANKED UP –
SO'S THE DRIVER.

'I thought you said your Archie was useless?'

'Not exactly – he often helps the police with
their inquiries.'

Two drunks at bus station. Says one: 'Ask
that copper if the last Liverpool bus has gone.'

So the drunk staggers over and says: 'Tell
me, constable, has the last bus to Liverpool
gone?'

'Yes,' says the copper, 'it left ages ago.'

'Thanks,' says the drunk, and breaks the
news to his pal.

'Ask him if the last Manchester bus has
gone,' he tells him.

So the drunk goes back to the policeman.
'Do you know if the last Manchester bus has
gone?'

'It has,' says the policeman, 'half an hour
ago.'

Again, the drunk goes back and puts his
mate in the picture.

'Ask him if the last bus to London has left,'
he murmurs.

The drunk goes back yet again. 'Has the last
bus to London gone, constable?'

'Yes, yes, yes,' shouts the constable.
'They've all gone.'

The drunk goes back and tells him the last
buses have all gone.

'Great,' says the other, 'it's safe to cross the road!'

Sean met Michael in the street. Michael was carrying a crate of Guinness.
    'Going to a party?' asks Sean.
    'No,' replies Michael, 'moving house.'

Some people have no respect for age, unless it's bottled.

PubTalkPubTalkPubTalkPubTalkPubTalk

'The doctor says I've only three weeks to live.'
    'Don't worry – it'll soon pass.'

'Gloria? She can be had for a song.'
    'Aye – the Wedding March.'

'How's that brother of yours who fell into the upholstery machine?'
    'Him? He's fully recovered.'

'My son's going through a rough period – changing from a hooligan to a layabout.'

'I once tried to give up smoking, gambling, drinking and women.'
    'Really?'
    'Yes – it was the longest day I ever spent.'

Paul a heavy drinker? You must be joking! He didn't know the water was cut off for two months.'

'My brother – he was an only child.'

A feller came into a bar with a fried egg on his head and ordered a pint of beer. The barman handed it over and asked: 'Don't think I'm being curious, but why have you got a fried egg on your head?'

'Well, it's like this,' explained the chap, 'the boiled ones keep rolling off.'

What's the difference between an Aberdonian and a coconut?

You can get a drink out of a coconut.

A man went to his doctor because his hands kept shaking.

The doctor gave him a thorough examination. 'Tell me,' he asked, 'do you drink much?'

'No,' replied the man, 'I spill most of it.'

One reason why elephants drink so much water is because no one offers them anything else.

This Jewish landlord of a pub picks up the phone and a voice says: 'There's a 50 lb bomb in the bar. It'll go off in ten minutes.' The landlord puts the phone down and shouts: 'Last orders, please!'

Definition of a hangover: the wrath of grapes.

This drunk flops in a train beside a priest and starts reading a newspaper. 'Tell me, Father,' he says after a bit, 'what causes arthritis?'

Says the priest with relish: 'I'll tell you what causes arthritis ... loose living, going with cheap women, and, above all, too much alcohol. Tell me – how long have you had arthritis?'

'I don't have arthritis,' replies the drunk, 'but it says here that the Pope has.'

Amazing what a big pools win can do to a man. Charlie is leading the Campaign For Real Champagne.

Said the drunk to the barmaid: 'I've three dolly birds in the corner who are mine for tonight. Give us three large gins, miss.'

'Don't you "miss" me!' snapped the barmaid.

'OK, darling – make it four large gins, then.'

The tipsy bride was making a thank-you speech for the presents: 'And I'd like to thank my parents-in-law for giving me such a perky copulator!'

Confucius say: 'Drunk man smother wife with kisses. Sober man use pillow.'

This drunk in the cinema was asked by the attendant to move seats and adamantly refused. So the manager was called.

'Look,' he said, 'are you going to move your seat or not?'

'I'm staying right where I am,' said the drunk.

'Very well,' said the manager, 'when the organ goes up – *you play*!'

Two drunks in bar. 'What's the date, Jimmy?' asks one.

'Dunno – look at the newspaper in your pocket.'

'Naw, that's nae use – it's yesterday's.'

A drunk wanders out of the pub, stops a man in the street, and asks him for 50p for a cup of coffee.

'Here's £3,' says the man, in generous mood, 'get yourself half a dozen cups.'

Next day, the drunk accosts the man again. 'You and your six cups of coffee,' he complains. 'They kept me awake all night!'

'My wife hates drink. She used to say: "Lips that touch drink will never touch mine." '

'So?'

'I haven't kissed her for fifteen years.'

PubTalkPubTalkPubTalkPubTalkPubTalk

'You've a wife in a million, Arthur.'

'I know – I just wish she was normal like everyone else.'

'For twelve years, Ronnie, I didn't know what sex was.'

'Get away!'

'But when I was thirteen ... '

'Lend me a tenner for a month old boy.'

'What does a month-old boy want with a tenner?'

'I eat in a different restaurant every day.'

'I don't tip either.'

'How's your pain in the neck?'
  'She's staying with her mother.'

'Why do you call your mother-in-law The Exorcist?'
  'Every Christmas she comes and gets rids of all the spirits.'

'Are you married, John?'
  'No – I was hit by a car.'

Two men in a pub. 'I wouldn't go to America if you paid me,' says one.
  'Why's that?'
  'Well, for one thing, they drive on the right-hand side of the road.'
  'What's wrong with that?'
  'I tried it the other day and it's bloody dangerous.'

Pub graffiti: THIRST COME, THIRST SERVED.

Then there was the drunk who felt like sobering up, so he rang Irish Alcoholics Anonymous. Five minutes later, a chap came round with a crate of Guinness.

'I'm thinking of divorcing Wilfred,' the wife told her friend in the snug.

'For why?'

'He smokes in bed.'

'Surely smoking in bed isn't a sufficient reason?'

'*Bacon?*'

Pub sign: 'Don't laugh at our beer. You may be old and weak yourself one day.'

Two heavy drinkers went fishing. As they got in the boat, one asked: 'What did you bring for lunch?'

Says the other: 'Ten packs of beer and half a dozen buttered biscuits.'

Says the first: 'What in the world do you expect to do with all those biscuits?'

This guy in the pub complained his wife's living bra had died of malnutrition.

What do you call a Scotsman who's been banned from his local pub?

Homesick.

After an accident on the M1, a police sergeant asked the driver: 'Would you please blow in this bag, sir? It tells you whether you've had too much to drink.'

'Really?' said the driver. 'I'm married to one of them!'

Said the drunk as he staggered into his house in the early hours: 'Am I home, darling?'

How about the two newly ordained priests who went on the town to celibate?

It was talent night in the pub, and a local was giving *When Irish Eyes Are Smiling* his all. Which made one woman put her handkerchief to her eyes to wipe away a tear or two.

Thinking she was emotionally overcome, a chap placed his hand sympathetically on her shoulder and asked: 'Tell me — are you Irish, then?'

'No,' came the reply. 'I'm a music teacher.'

Men have always two good reasons for staying out drinking all night. Either they've got no wives to go home to, or they have.

A drunk saw a rag and bone man trying to adjust a nosebag on a lively horse. 'You'll never do it, pal, you'll never do it,' said the drunk.

'Do what?'

'You'll never put that big horse in that little bag.'

This boozer walks over Westminster Bridge, puts 2p in a post box, looks up at Big Ben and says: 'Christ, I've lost some weight!'

How about the chap in the pub who drank eight Cokes and burped 7-Up?

Sid stopped off at the pub on his way home, met a beautiful blonde, and had a few jars.

Near closing time, she said: 'How about coming back to my place, love?'

'I'd love to,' murmured Sid, 'but what about the wife?'

'Don't worry,' assured the blonde. 'Leave everything to me.'

So they went back to her apartment and had a wonderful time. At four in the morning, Sid said: 'Bloody hell – look at the time. What do I tell the missus?'

'No problem,' said the blonde. 'Just tell her the truth. Oh – and stick this bit of chalk behind your ear.'

So Sid wandered home ... to find his irate wife sitting in the hall, rolling pin in hand. 'Where do you think YOU'VE been to this ungodly hour?' she asked.

'I cannot tell a lie,' replied Sid. 'I stopped off for a drink in the pub, met this beautiful blonde, went back to her place, and we made mad, passionate love.'

'Don't come home with a story like that,' she stormed. 'You've been out playing snooker with your mates again – I can tell by that chalk behind your ear!'

Pub graffiti: LIQUOR IS SLOW POISON – WHO'S IN A HURRY?

Then there was the Glasgow pub that advertised for dwarf barmen ... for serving customers who drink themselves under the table.

Sign over pub grub: 'Do not touch the food.'

A white horse was feeling thirsty, so he went into a bar and asked the barman if he could recommend a drink.

'Why not have the whisky named after you?' asked the barman.

'Very well,' said the horse, 'I'll have a double Eric.'

Every Friday night, regular as clockwork, Charlie would leave his wife and family, hop into his car, and join his pals at the local for a few drinks.

One night he went off as usual, and didn't come back for seven years. His wife was so happy to see him that she called up her friends to come and celebrate.

'Wait a minute,' said Charlie, 'what exactly is going on?'

'I'm just having a few friends over in honour of your return,' explained his wife.

'Oh, really?' growled Charlie, *on my night out?*

Two drunks in a bar. 'You should have been here last night,' said one. 'There was a chap in here selling Rothmans cigarettes at £1.50. for a million.'

Said the second: 'Why didn't you get me twenty?'

'Tough luck on Willie. He missed his alimony last month.'

'What happened?'

'His wife repossessed him.'

This drunk was hurling a hedgehog against a brick wall, when a policeman came along.

'What do you think you're doing?' asked the copper.

'Not a lot,' replied the drunk, 'I'm only trying to get out the conker.'

Pub sign: 'If you're driving, be sure you have a car.'

A drunk at a wedding asked where the men's room was. He was told it was at the end of the corridor, turn left, and open the first door.

He went down the corridor, turned *right*, opened the first door – and fell down the lift shaft.

When he got to the bottom, he looked up and shouted: 'For God's sake, don't flush it!'

Definition of high fidelity: A drunk who goes home regularly to his wife.

'Have you trained that dog of yours, Jimmy?'

'Too true. I have only to say "attack" and he has one.'

Pub graffiti: ABSTINENCE IS THE THIN EDGE OF THE PLEDGE.

The landlord of this pub was a West Ham fanatic. He put up a sign saying: 'No Arsenal fans served in this pub.'

One day, a chap wearing Arsenal colours rushed in, desperate for a drink. 'I know you don't serve Arsenal supporters,' he said, 'but I'll give you a fiver for a pint.'

The landlord thought it over and decided to serve the beer, which the fan downed in one. 'Same again,' he said.

'That'll cost you a tenner,' said the landlord. The man paid up, then asked for a third pint. 'Fifteen pounds,' said the landlord, and rang up the money.

When the Arsenal fan had gone, the landlord put up a new sign: '*Only* Arsenal fans served in this pub.'

This drunk in the hotel lobby bet he could whip anybody in the place. The elevator man took him up.

Spare a thought for the man in the pub who died drinking a pint of Longlife.

'This suit was a present from the wife.'
  'A surprise, was it?'
  'Yes – I came home early from the pub one night and found it lying on the bed.'

PubTalkPubTalkPubTalkPubTalkPubTalk

'My hubby's left me a farewell note.'
  'Yes, but he always comes back.'
  'Not this time – he's taken his darts board.'

'What's that bump on your head, Bert?'
  'Only a glancing blow – the wife caught me glancing at another bird.'

'Didn't your wife mind you staying out fishing all weekend?'
  'Naw – I was going to have my front teeth out, anyway.'

'Was it you or your twin brother that got buried at sea?'

'Why do they call him Palistrano?'
  'He's always ready for a few swallows.'

'Tommy's taken up jogging.'
  'Yes … he always would run a mile rather than buy a round.'

'My wife's an angel.'
  'You're lucky – mine's still alive.'

A drunk was leaning against the front door of a house, when a policeman came along. 'What's the problem?' he asked.

'It's all right, constable,' said the drunk, 'I live here.'

'Then why not go in?'

'I've lost my key.'

'There are lights showing – why not ring?'

'I have rung.'

'Then ring again.'

'Not likely – let 'em wait!'

Heard about the chap in the pub they call Joe Bugner? He never gets a round in.

Three soccer fans stagger into a bar near closing time. One collapses on the floor. The others order a double Scotch each.

'What about him?' asks the barman, pointing to the legless chap on the floor.

'Oh, no more for him,' says one, 'he's driving.'

'Hey, Angus, I'll buy the first round – you can't call me mean. What'll you have?'

'Half a pint of bitter, Jock.'

'What, a FULL half?'

The difference between being an alcoholic and a plain drunk is that a drunk doesn't have to attend all those damned meetings.

What do you call an Irishman who steals your drink? Nick McGuinness.

Two wizened old men were being interviewed in the bar lounge by a reporter. 'How old are you, sir?' the first man was asked.

'I'm ninety-five next birthday, and I owe it all to clean living, early to bed, no cigarettes, and half a pint of beer a week.'

Turning to the second man, the reporter asked: 'How about you, sir?'

The man coughed and wheezed. 'I drink a bottle of Scotch a day, chain-smoke cigarettes, take no exercise, and I carry on with women.'

'And how old are you?'

'Twenty-seven.'

This chap in the pub was trying to carry back four pints, three whiskies, two vodkas and a bottle of lemonade, when the barman offered him a tray. 'No thanks,' he said, 'I've enough to carry without that!'

Definition of High Noon: three double brandies before lunch.

This drinker sat glumly at the bar, nursing a pint. 'What's the problem?' asked the barman.

'Well,' said the punter, 'two months ago, my grandfather died and left me £50,000.'

'Well?'

'And last month an uncle I'd never even met left me £35,000.'

'So why the sad look?'

'Well, this month, so far – *nothing*!'

A pub is the only place where you say cheers when they greet you with booze.

Then there was the bar tender who asked for overtime pay – time and a fifth.

After closing time, a drunk staggered into the pizza parlour next door and suddenly remembered what day it was. 'Say,' he asked the assistant, 'could you put "Happy Birthday" on this pizza?'

How about the suicidal seal that flip-flopped into a bar and asked for a Canadian Club on the rocks?

This drunk staggers into the Fire Station with a penguin stuck to his head.

'Can I help you?' asked the firemaster.

'Yes,' said the penguin, 'get this man off my feet.'

Police caught a drunk climbing over the wall at a Chelsea match. They escorted him back into the ground.

As a lorryload of turf went by, one drunk said to his pal: 'That's what I would do if I won the pools.'

'What's that, Jimmy?'

'Send my grass away to be cut.'

Judge: 'Do you recognize this court?'

Drunk: 'Not since it's been decorated.'

How about the man who went into an Interflora shop and tried to send a crate of Flowers beer to his brother-in-law?

Then there was the chap who suffered from alcoholic rheumatism. He got stiff in all the joints.

Two pensioners in a pub. 'Do you remember them pills they used to give us in the Army to keep our minds off the girls?'

'Aye, come to think of it, I do.'

'Well, you know what — I think mine are beginning to work.'

This temperance lady was carrying out a survey of drinking habits. She knocked at a house and a man answered.

'I'm doing a survey into people's drinking habits,' she said. 'Would you mind giving me some information about yours?'

'Not at all,' came the reply. 'I haven't had a drink since — let me see — 1945.'

'Really? That's quite an achievment.'

'Oh, I don't know — it's 20.00 now.'

A pretty nurse came into the pub lounge, selling poppies. 'Buy a poppy, sir?' she asked one punter.

'I'll give you a fiver for one,' he said, 'if you promise to nurse me should I ever go into your hospital.'

'It's a bargain,' said the nurse, handing the poppy over.

'By the way,' said the punter, 'which hospital do you work in?'

'St Catherine's maternity,' came the reply.

Then a Salvation Army man wandered in.
'How about a *War Cry*?' he asked.
　　And a drunk shouted 'Geronimo!'

PubTalkPubTalkPubTalkPubTalkPubTalk

'What do the newscasters say at the end of
News at Ten?'
　　' "If we hurry, we might be just in time for a
drink." '

'I'm a self-made man.'
　　'I accept your apology.'

'Jimmy – your jacket's on fire.'
　　'It's all right – it's a smoking jacket.'

'My missus drives me to drink.'
　　'You're lucky – I have to walk to the pub.'

'Is your separation permanent, Madge?'
　　'Yes – I poisoned him.'

'He's going to sing a song he wrote himself.'
　　'Good of him to take the blame.'

'Is that hand-knitted?'
　　'No – it came with my arm.'

This Aberdonian won a new car in a raffle. Yet
he was sititng in the pub, looking miserable as
sin.

'What's up, Jock?' asked his pal.

'Och,' came the reply, 'it's this other raffle ticket.'

'What about it?'

'I canna imagine why I ever bought it.'

Two drunks staggering down the street come to a bus garage.

Says one: 'Let's pinch a bus to get home.'

Says the other: 'We'll never get ours out — it's right at the back.'

Three pieces of string walk up to the bar. One orders a round, but the barman says 'Get out!' The second one does the same and gets a similar response.

Left on its own, the third piece of string — a right dishevelled, twisted lot — asks for a pint.

The barman says: 'Look, pal, aren't you a piece of string as well?'

And the string replies: *'I'm a frayed knot!'*

How about the alcoholic bellringer who woke up next morning with a shocking clangover?

This drunk goes up to a copper in the road. 'Tell me, constable, where's the other side of the street?'

'That's it over there.'

'I thought as much. Some swine told me this is it!'

Things were bad at this pub in Barnsley. They even employed a chucker-in!

1st drunk: 'When I was born, I weighed only 3½ lbs.'

2nd drunk: 'Did you live?'

1st drunk: 'Did I? You should see me now!'

The Irish have invented a new kind of bomb. It kills people but leaves the pubs standing.

A drunk approaches a statistician in the street. 'Give us a handout, guv,' he pleads. 'I haven't eaten for three days.'

'Really?' says the statistician with interest. 'Tell me ... how does that compare with the same period last year?'

Then there was the chap who joined Alcoholics Anonymous. He never went to the meetings. He used to drink and send in the empties.

The Salvation Army man in the pub warned Charlie: 'If you continue drinking as you do, you'll get smaller and smaller, and turn into a mouse.'

So a scared Charlie went home and told his wife: 'Sarah ... if you notice me getting smaller and smaller – kill that damned cat!'

Confucius say: Spend money on drink rather than women. You can always hold a pint up to the light to see what you're getting.

Pub graffiti: I'VE TOO MUCH BLOOD IN MY ALCOHOL STREAM.

Hubby, on phone in pub to wife: 'I know I said I'd be home after six – but I haven't finished my fourth yet.'

Drunk at registry office: 'Gentlemen ... my wife had twin sons this morning and I want to register them. Have a cigar.'

'Thank you, sir. But why the "gentlemen"? There's only myself here.'

'In that case,' came the reply, 'I'd better go back and have another look.'

The barman looked up casually as a couple of pink elephants and a mauve giraffe walked in. 'Sorry, lads,' he said, 'Willie hasn't been in this evening.'

Two men enter a pub and sit down at the bar. 'Two pints of cider,' says one, laying down a couple of bottle tops as payment.

The second man murmurs to the barman: 'Don't mind him – he's a bit round the twist. Just play him along and I'll settle up later.'

So the barman serves them drinks till closing time, when the pair rise unsteadily to leave.

'Just a minute,' says the barman to the second drinker, 'I thought you were going to settle up?'

'So I am,' he replies, producing a dustbin lid. 'Here – take it out of that, and have one for yourself.'

This drunk went to the doctor for a check-up. 'I'm afraid your health's not too good,' said the doctor. 'You'll have to give up certain things.'

'What sort of things, doc?'

'Well, wine and women, for a start. But you can *sing* as much as you want.'

Then there was the chappie who ordered a pint of beer from the wood and ended up with a splinter in his tongue.

A feller bounds into the bar. 'The drinks are on me,' he says. 'I've just sold the house – £35,000.'

'Great stuff,' say the others, placing their orders.

'Mind you,' he adds, 'the council will go mad when they find out.'

A chap came out of the pub at closing time, got into his car and was weaving all over the road. A police car drew up. 'Let's have a look at your licence,' says the sergeant.

The driver handed it over, and the sergeant said: 'This isn't a driving licence – it's a shooting licence.'

'I know,' said the driver. 'This is a shooting brake, isn't it?'

Pub graffiti: CONSERVE WATER – DILUTE IT.

Then there was the man with no legs who stayed on in the pub after closing time. He explained he was waiting for a carry-out.

An Aberdonian, picked up for drunk driving, refused to give a blood sample. He said he didn't think he could spare that much.

A drunk, helped by his pal, staggered into a temperance hotel. 'You can't bring him in here,' shouted the proprietor.

'It's all right,' replied his pal, 'he's too far gone to notice!'

1st salesman: 'Why are you having a bar lunch instead of your usual five courses in the hotel? Are you on a diet?'

2nd salesman: 'No – on commission.'

Sign in pub: 'Please don't throw your cigarette ends on the floor, as they may burn the customers leaving on their hands and knees.'

This feller's mother-in-law kept a pub called the George and Dragon.

A little bloke came in one night and went up to the bar. She glared at him and bawled: 'Well ... ?'

And the little chap said: 'Is George in?'

Then there was the punter who took a ladder to the party because he heard drinks were on the house.

PubTalkPubTalkPubTalkPubTalkPubTalk

'Do you serve women in this bar?'
  'No, sir, you must bring your own.'

'That Bristol Cream did absolutely nothing for my bust, Madge.'

'That whisky will be £2.30, Mac.'
  'If you'd charged like that at Bannockburn, you'd have won.'

'Maureen, do you prefer men who drink or the other kind?'
  'What other kind?'

'If I had my life to live again, I'd start making the same mistakes sooner.'

'What do you take for a headache?'
  'Booze the night before.'

'How long have you been wearing a corset, Jack?'
  'Ever since the wife found it in the car.'

'How many fags do you smoke in a day?'
  'Any given amount.'

An American tourist was hiking in the Highlands of Scotland when he came upon a pub hidden in the hills, which was packed out with customers having one helluva time. There was singing and dancing to a fiddle band, and the drinks were flowing non-stop.

As the evening wore on, the American had a word with the landlord. 'This is some pub,' he said. 'I've never seen so many people having such a good time. When's closing time?'

And the landlord replied: 'October.'

SCHOOLBOY HOWLERS

Guinnesses is the first book of the Bible.

To be 'called to the Bar' is to be treated to a drink.

The blood consists of red and white corkscrews.

A brewery is a place where beer is buried.

A chap was in the pub with his wife. Near closing time, he said: 'I think you've had enough.'

'What do you mean?' asked his wife.

'Your face is getting blurred.'

Sign outside pub: 'Good clean entertainment every night except Monday.'

'Hey, landlord, this beer tastes like tepid rainwater.'
'Look, pal, you've only got a pint – I've twenty-seven barrels of the stuff!'

PubTalkPubTalkPubTalkPubTalkPubTalk

'She's like a sparkling wine – gets right up my nose.'

'There's a fly in my glass of wine, barman.'
'Well, you asked for a drink with a little body in it.'

'I tried contact lenses, but I couldn't get them over my glasses.'

'This getting up and going to work every morning breaks up my whole day.'

'He's bi-sexual. If he can't get it, he buys it.'

'Jack's got absorbing qualities. He sponges off everyone he meets.'

'The wife's just left me.'
'Really? How much?'

'Jock had his toes amputated so he could stand nearer the bar.'

'I drink to forget, but I've forgotten why.'

'Sam drank so much the Customs bonded his liver.'

Drunk to landlord: 'Hey, Jimmy, tell me one thing.'
   'What's that?'
   'Why don't you buy yourself a watch? Then you wouldn't have to keep shouting "Time, gentlemen, please." '

How about the drinker who was addicted to Harpic? He went clean round the bend.

Two termites walk into a pub. One asks: 'Is the bar tender here?'

Sign over wine display in shop window: 'This is the Beaune that's worth working your fingers to.'

This chap went on a weekend drinking spree, and couldn't think of an excuse to tell his wife.

Finally, he phoned her from the pub and said: 'Don't pay the ransom money, darling – I've escaped!'

This Birmingham chap in Abu Dhabi got a hundred lashes. Well, they *told* him it wasn't a good idea to open a pub.

Pub graffiti: DRINK WET CEMENT AND GET REALLY STONED.

A drunk was sobbing in the car park of this pub. 'What's the matter?' asked a passer-by.

'Someone's pinched my hoop,' cried the drunk.

'Don't worry – I expect the police will find it in the morning.'

'That's all right ... *but how am I going to get home tonight?*'

How about the boozer who scoffed three and a half pounds of peanuts one night? He was done for assault.

'What time is it, constable?' asked the drunk in the street.

'It's one o'clock in the morning,' replied the copper, and hit him once over the head.

'Bloody hell,' said the drunk, 'I'm glad I didn't ask you an hour ago!'

A feller came home late from the pub, and his wife complained he never took her anywhere. Next morning at 6.30 he gave her a nudge in bed and said: 'Fancy coming to work with me?'

Then there was the punter who helped out in the drought of 1983 by drinking dry Martinis.

This bar had a big bottle full of 10p pieces. Said the barman: 'If anyone can guess the number of 10p pieces in this jar, he can have them.'

All the customers had a go, without success. Then this drunk pipes up: 'I'll say two thousand pieces.'

'You're absolutely right,' said the barman, and hands the jar over.

The drunk staggers home, clutching this jar. Just as he's going inside his house, the bottle slips and all the 10p pieces go here, there and everywhere. The drunk decides to go to bed and pick them up the next day.

111

In the morning, his wife wakes him up. 'Guess what's on the doorstep,' she says.

'Don't tell me,' comes the reply, 'two thousand 10p pieces.'

'No,' says the wife, 'a thousand bottles of milk.'

A man walked into this bar with a Chihuahua dog on a lead. 'Sorry,' said the landlord, 'you can't bring a dog in here.'

'But you don't understand,' protested the man. 'I'm blind – this is a guide dog.'

'You must be joking,' said the landlord, 'that's a Chihuahua.'

'Oh, really?' came the reply. 'I thought it was an Alsatian!'

Sign seen during beer strike in Dublin: 'Don't waste time going to your local. It's pintless.'

A SHAGGY CAT STORY

A pianist was playing away in this pub, when one of the customers shouted: 'What a load of rubbish. I've a tom cat in the car that can play better than that.'

'All right,' said the pianist, 'if he's that good, why don't you bring him in?'

So the chap goes out and returns with this cat, which he puts on the piano stool. 'He's going to play a number he wrote for Cat Stevens,' says the owner.

When the cat had finished, the publican says: 'That was marvellous. What a song! Why don't you get it orchestrated?'

At that, the tom cat jumped off the stool and was never seen again.

The Irish are great believers in health. They're always drinking to other people's.

Graffiti: ALCOHOL A PROBLEM? JOIN THE AA AND DRIVE AWAY FROM IT.

Then there was the ventriloquist who asked the barman for a gottle of gear. He drank it without moving his lips.

Men makes passes at girls who drain glasses.

'What did the doctor have to say, Willie?'

'He said he had some bad news and some very bad news.'

'What was the bad news?'

'I've only three weeks to live.'
'And the very bad news?'
'He should have told me two weeks ago.'

Pub sign: 'Always borrow money from a pessimist. He doesn't expect to be paid back.'

A chap and his dog were sitting at a bar. He ordered two Martinis, drank one and gave the other to the dog.

The animal drank it in one go, ate the glass till only the base remained, and walked out.

'That's the daftest thing I've ever seen,' commented the barman.

'Yes, he's a dumb son of a bitch,' said the fellow. 'The base is the best part.'

This chap was driving down the road after having one over the eight. A police car waved him down. 'Didn't you see the 30 mph sign?' asked the sergeant.

'To tell you the truth – no,' came the reply. 'I was driving too fast.'

PUBTALKPUBTALKPUBTALKPUBTALKPUBTALK

'Does your hubby never get a hangover?'
'No, Elsie – he's always drunk.'

'Lazy? He even had his window box paved over.'

'Here comes the only woman who knows the news before Sue Lawley.'

'Why does your dog keep saying "meow," Hector?'
   'He's a police dog working under cover.'

'He's a right workaholic – mention work and he goes out and gets drunk.'

'Unlucky? If he'd been one of Raquel Welch's triplets ... he'd be the one that was bottle-fed.'

'Drink doesn't affect me. The only trouble is people keep stepping on my fingers.'

Did you hear about the latest Budget in Saudi Arabia? They put thirty lashes on a bottle of whisky.

'Hey, Sammy, you got drunk last night and sold me the Tower of London?'
   'So ... ?'
   'I bought it!'

A drunk was walking along the road when an Irish wolfhound knocked him down. Then a

Sinclair C5 car skidded round the corner and inflicted more damage.

A bystander, helping the drunk up, asked: 'Are you all right?'

'Well, the dog didn't hurt much,' replied the drunk, 'but that tin can tied to his tail nearly killed me!'

How about the Aberdeen farmer who laced his chicken feed with a bottle of Scotch? He hoped they'd lay Scotch Eggs.

'I'd a lovely idea for your birthday, Jack, but the packing was too much of a problem.'

'How do you mean?'

'Well, can you tell me how to wrap up a brewery?'

Sign in pub: 'Remember the customer is always tight.'

A fellow walked into a bar and ordered a beer and a whisky. He drank the beer and poured the whisky into his top pocket.

After repeating this routine several more times, the puzzled bar tender asked: 'What's the big idea?'

'It's none of your business,' retorted the

man. 'What's more, you're so nosy I've a good mind to punch you in the eye.'

At which a mouse popped his head out of the chap's top pocket and said: 'And that goes for your damned cat, too!'

Two drunks in a pub. 'This doctor said I'd only two weeks to live.'

'What did you say?'

'I'll take the first two weeks in August.'

This guest at the club dinner got hardly any wine all evening. When he proposed the toast to Absent Friends, he coupled it with the name of the wine waiter ...

An Aberdonian was arrested for breaking into a pound note in a pub. He was let off, as it was his first offence.

Drunk: 'What d'you mean, I'm a failure?'

Wife: 'I'll put it this way – ours is the only house in the street that hasn't been burgled.'

Then there was the boozer who liked to support sick animals. The trouble was he didn't know they were sick when he backed them.

'Hey, Dick, when you told your missus you'd be home late, what did she say?'
   'She said: "Can I depend on that?" '

My grandfather drank a bottle of rum every day from the age of seventeen. When he died seven years ago, aged ninety-five, they cremated him ... and they're still trying to put the fire out.

Two drunks in a bar.
   'This match won't light, Jimmy.'
   'Whassa matter with it?'
   'Dunno – it lit before.'

Christopher Lee's favourite tipple is a Bloody Mary – group 'O'.

How about the drunk who broke his arm at one party and his leg at another? He took out third party insurance.

Robert happened to be passing this pub. A barrel of beer fell from a lorry and sent him flying. Luckily, it was light ale.

A feller was stopped for speeding. 'According to our radar clock,' said the sergeant, 'you were travelling at ninety miles per hour.'

'Rubbish,' retorted the driver. 'I was only doing seventy.'

'You were doing ninety.'

'I tell you I was only doing seventy.'

At which point, his wife interjected: 'Don't argue with him, officer, when he's had a few drinks.'

'How much did your dog cost, Arthur?'

'Five hundred pounds ... he's part beagle and part bull.'

'Which part is bull?'

'The part about the five hundred pounds.'

Pub graffiti: W.C. FIELDS IS ALIVE AND DRUNK IN PHILADELPHIA.

PubTalkPubTalkPubTalkPubTalkPubTalk

'Talk about drink? He's listed in *Booze Who*.'

'I can't remember when my hubby's birthday is, but I think it's some time this year.'

'What d'you reckon I should get for the wife this Christmas?'
  'Dunno – a fiver?'

'Him? He joined twenty unions on the chance he'll always be on strike.'

'Yeh, the wife's pretty as a picture – if you like modern art.'

'What do you reckon caused the hangover?'
  'Too many slices of lemon last night.'

'They gave him a smashing funeral – took six strong men to carry the beer.'

'How's your man doing with his slimming diet?'
  'Wonderful – he disappeared last week.'

COCKTAIL HOUR

● The Mark Thatcher Cocktail ... one sip and you lose your sense of direction.

● The John McEnroe Cocktail ... one sip and you feel you're being harassed.

● The Larry Grayson Cocktail ... one sip and you're away with the fairies.

● The Chas & Dave Cocktail ... one sip and you're up the apples 'n' pears.

● The Chris Bonington Cocktail ... one sip and your head is in the clouds.

● The Lord Longford Cocktail ... one sip and you're begging everyone's pardon.

● The Ted Moult Cocktail ... one sip and you've got that double-glazed look.

● The Lorraine Chase Cocktail ... one sip and you don't arf feel good!

● The Barry Norman Cocktail ... one sip and you're baggy-eyed.

● The Val Doonican Cocktail ... one sip and you're off your rocker.

● The Cliff Richard Cocktail ... one sip and you're in Never-Never land.

● The Michael Fish Cocktail ... one sip and you're under the weather.

● The Russell Grant Cocktail ... one sip and you're seeing stars.

● The Barry McGuigan Cocktail ... one sip and you're out for the count.

● The Paul Daniels Cocktail ... one sip and you're bewildered – not a lot!

● The Grace Jones Cocktail ... one sip and you throw the rest in someone's face.

This fellow in the bar orders four pints, three Scotches, and half a dozen packets of crisps.
   'That'll be £8.75,' says the barman.
   'Is an Irish tenner all right?' asks the chap.
   'No problem,' replied the bar tender.
   So the punter breaks out into 'Oh, Danny Boy ... '

Then there was the Glasgow pub that hired a famous entertainer to knock down a pile of drunks.

Sign in the Irish Samaritans: 'Happy hour, 5.30-6.30 pm.'

This feller comes home and says to his wife: 'Let's go down the pub and celebrate.'
   'What have we got to celebrate?' asks his wife.
   'After ten months on the dole, I've got a job at last.'
   'Oh, no,' says his wife, 'just when we were getting on our feet.'

Irish cocktail: Perrier and water.

Pub graffiti: A MARS BAR IS AN INTER-PLANETARY PUB.

Then there was the punter who thought the *Guinness Book of Records* was an LP of Irish drinking songs.

A Glasgow chap goes into a bar in Lambeth and asks for a pint of beer and a packet of crisps.

The barman hands the beer over, and opens the crisps on the counter.

'Awannasot,' says the Scot hoarsely.

'Sorry?' says the barman.

'Awannasot,' repeats the punter.

'Ah,' says the barman, 'you want the salt. I thought you were one short!'

'What'll you have, Albert?'

'A Harvey Smith.'

'What's that?'

'Two fingers of Scotch.'

Then there was the drunk who found he was overdrawn at the bottle bank.

Sad about the Dublin brewery that went up in flames. Eighteen men were burnt to death jumping in.

These two blokes in the bar are talking about cars. 'I wish I could sell mine,' says one, 'but nobody wants to know.'

'How many miles on the clock?' asks the other.

'Three hundred and fifty thousand.'

'Why don't you turn back the clock?'

'That's a good idea.'

The following week they met again in the pub. 'Did you manage to sell the car?' asks the second chap.

Replies the other: 'Why should I want to sell a car that's only done fifteen thousand miles?'

Pub graffiti: DUTCH COURAGE IS AN AMSTERDAM BEER.

This old chap was sitting in a corner in the pub, reading *Hollywood Wives* and crying his eyes out.

'What's the problem?' asks the landlord.

'I'm reading *Hollywood Wives*,' comes the reply.

'But *Hollywood Wives* isn't a sad book.'

'It is when you get to my age!'

A pity about the landlord who fell off the roof of his pub. A customer had told him to put the drinks on the slate.

PubTalkPubTalkPubTalkPubTalkPubTalk

'I'm going on a ski holiday.'

'I don't like yoghurt.'

'Yes, he's a model husband. Unfortunately he's not a working model.'

'Did you book any special place for the wife's holiday?'

'No – I told the fellow anywhere in the Bermuda Triangle.'

'Don't you think of anything else but booze?'

'Yes, but I fight it.'

'I hear your lad left school.'

'Yeh, it won't make much difference. He didn't go when he went, anyway.'

'Are the Clancy Brothers really brothers?'

'Yes – and so are the Nolan Sisters.'

'She carries her age well.'

'She should – she's had years of experience.'

'Look, dear,' said the drunk brightly, staggering into the hall, 'another beer mat for our collection!'

This punter arrived home from the pub early and found his wife in bed. A large cigar was smouldering in the ashtray.

'Where the hell did that cigar come from?' he asked suspiciously.

And, from the wardrobe, a shaky male voice answered: 'Cuba!'

How about the landlord who advertised a TOPLESS BAR? It had no roof.

He whispered in her ear in the pub lounge: 'How about joining me for a quiet weekend in a country hotel?'

She: 'I'm afraid that my awareness of your proclivities in the esoteric aspects of sexual behaviour precludes such an erotic confrontation.'

He: 'I don't get it.'

She: 'Exactly.'

'Charlie, I should never have got married.'

'Why not?'

'The wife hates me when I'm drunk, and I can't stand the sight of her when I'm sober.'

A drunk is staggering down the street with a nun on each side lending a helping hand. Suddenly, he blinks, does a double-take, and says: 'Good grief – how did you do that?'

This pub had a sign 'Bar food at popular prices.'

A feller walks in, orders a pint and a couple of ham sandwiches, and the bartender charges him £7.65.

The punter points to the sign. 'I thought it says bar food at popular prices?'

'Well,' replies the barman, 'I like 'em!'

Bernard used to tell stories in the pub of a relative of his ... could drink twelve pints of Guinness, half a bottle of rum, a bottle of whisky, six large brandies, and wipe the floor with four strong men. Wonderful woman, she was.

Aberdonian to barman in empty club bar: 'Ah've just had a hole in one – drinks all round!'

On a pub wall: 'THE GRAFFITI IN THIS PUB IS TERRIBLE.' Below, someone scrawled 'So is the shepherd's pie.'

Two drunks in a pub. One cups his hands and says: 'Guess what I'm holding.'
  'An elephant.'
  'Try again.'
  'A steamroller.'
  'Have another guess.'
  'A flying saucer.'
  The first drunk bursts into tears. 'You peeked!' he says.

The man who enters a bar very optimistically often comes out very misty optically.

As Sean staggers home from the pub, he comes across a leprechaun trapped under a stone, and frees it.

'Thank you,' says the leprechaun, 'as a reward, name your three wishes.'

'I'll have a bottle of stout,' says Sean, and, sure enough, the bottle materializes.

'What's your second wish?'

'I wish this bottle would never be empty.'

'Granted,' says the leprechaun, 'and your third wish?'

'Well, now,' says Sean, waving his bottle, 'I'll be having another of these!'

Pub graffiti: GOING STEADY ONLY MEANS YOU SOBERED UP.

How about the drunk who was cured by a new wonder drug with an unusual side effect? His picture was on Page 3 of the *Sun* last week.

'I don't know who lives there,' said the drunk, passing the Post Office, 'but they get a helluva lot of letters.'

Two boozers were leaving the pub, when they spotted a copper looking suspiciously over their car.

'Did you change the plates over likes I told you?' asks one.

'Yes,' replies the other. 'I put the front plate

on the back and the back plate on the front.'

One night this chap staggers home, drunk as usual, to be met by his wife with her coat on. 'Come with me,' she says grimly. 'I've something to show you.'

And she takes him down to the brewery, which is ablaze with lights.

'Take a look at that,' she says. 'They're making it faster than you can drink it.'

'Yes,' replies the feller, 'but I've got them on the night shift!'

Man to hotel porter: 'I know it's five in the morning, but could you let me have a drop of whisky?'

'What on earth would you be wanting with whisky at this hour?'

'Soda.'

A lonely Scotsman, on his first visit to London is befriended in a pub by a Cockney. 'Where are you from, mate?' asks the Londoner.

'Arbroath,' replies the Scot, a frustrated football fan.

'Come again?' says the perplexed Cockney.

'Arbroath,' repeats the Scot. 'You'll know it better as Arbroath Nil.'

This drunk on the train told the ticket collector he'd bought a ticket but couldn't find it.

'It doesn't matter,' said the inspector, 'I'm sure you've paid.'

'It *does* matter,' exclaimed the drunk. 'Without my ticket, I don't know where I'm going!'

A drunk phones the fire station: 'Quick, quick, there's a fire!'

'Where is it?'

'At my house, of course.'

'I mean the *location*.'

'In the kitchen.'

'Yes, but how do we get to your place?'

'You've got a flippin' fire engine, haven't you?'

Two pals in a pub with a pig. 'This pig is a marvel,' says one. 'It saved my life once when the house was on fire. Another time it pulled me out of the river when I was drowning. And only last week, it rescued me from a blazing car.'

'That's amazing,' says the other. 'Tell me – why has it only one leg?'

'Well,' replies his pal, 'you don't eat a pig like that all at once!'

How about the drunk whose blood group was discontinued?

'I thought you said this was a theme pub, Bob?'

'So it is – the theme is getting pissed.'

A couple of dogs in a pub. 'What's your name?' asks one.

'I'm not sure,' replies the other, 'but I think it must be Down Boy.'

Lawyer to policeman in court: 'The fact that a man is on his hands and knees in the middle of the road doesn't prove he was drunk.'

'Agreed,' said the copper, 'but this punter was trying to roll up the white line!'

The best way to pull yourself out of your trouble is with a corkscrew.

Two drunks are staggering home from the pub. 'Come home to my house and have something to eat,' says one.

'It's two o'clock in the morning,' says the other. 'Your wife'll be mad.'

'Rubbish,' says the first. 'I've got the best wife in the world.'

So the two of them roll up to the house ... to be met by the wife wielding a rolling pin.

'You *have* got the best wife in the world,' says the other. 'You don't see many people baking at this time of night!'

Sign on Irish pub door: 'Gone to lunch. Back in half an hour. PS. Already gone twenty minutes.'

'Hey, Charlie, I hear there's a wife-swapping party down the road on Saturday. Shall we go?'

'Don't be daft, Albert. Who'd have mine?'

A man walked into a bar, saw a boomerang on the wall, and swallowed it. The landlord threw him out ... fifty-seven times.

'I'm Murphy – Irish and proud of it.'

'I'm MacPherson – Scotch and fond of it.'

This drunk in the police station was looking at the 'Wanted' pictures on the wall. 'What are they, sergeant?' he asked curiously.

'Them's pictures of wanted criminals,' replied the sergeant.

Retorted the drunk: 'Why didn't you keep hold of them when you took the pictures?'

Two men in the saloon bar. 'Did you hear about poor Frankie?'

'No – what happened?'

'He fell downstairs and broke six legs.'

'*Six* legs?'

'He was carrying the dog at the time.'

Pub graffiti: SMOKING SHORTENS YOUR CIGARETTES.

Copper: 'I'm going to ask you to accompany me to the station.'

Drunk: 'Why – don't you like walking there on your own?'

When this punter staggered home drunk, his wife was crying her eyes out. 'I baked a cake,' she sobbed, 'and the cat ate it all up.'

'Don't worry, pet,' he replied, 'I'll get you a new cat.'

'How did you celebrate your twenty-ninth anniversary?'
  'Two minutes' silence.'

'If George Best doesn't give up drinking, he'll end up playing for Fulham.'

'How did the accident happen, Jimmy?'
  'The wife fell asleep in the back seat.'

'Ah haven't a penny to my name.'
  'Change your name.'

'Of course we're incompatible, but she's far more incompatible than I am.'

'How did you get the black eye, Fred?'
  'I was hit by a guided muscle.'

'I always know when I've had enough – I stop moaning about the price.'

'That's a nice pleated shirt, Jack.'
  'It's not pleated – it's the way the wife irons.'

After a few drinks, this feller threatened to throw himself in the Mersey. 'I really mean it,' he shouted. 'I'm going to end it all. I don't want anyone to save me.' And he jumped in the water.
  A chap who was watching jumped in after

him. 'I told you – I don't want anyone to save me,' yelled the chap.

'I don't wanna save you,' replied the other, *'where do you work?'*

Heard about the drinker with a faulty pacemaker? Every time he burped, the garage door opened.

Then there was the chap who raises St Bernards just for the brandy.

'What did the doctor say, Arthur?'

'He couldn't diagnose my case, but he thought it was drink.'

'What then?'

'I told him I'd come back when he was sober.'

This barmaid had been patted so many times she has a cauliflower rear.

Notice in pub: 'If you can read this, you're upside down.'

After a night in the pub, Bert and Charlie staggered back to Bert's house. Feeling hungry, they took a 4 lb steak from the fridge and left in on the kitchen table, while they went inside for a couple of whiskies.

On their return, the steak had gone, and the cat was sitting in the corner, happily licking his whiskers.

'I'll bet that bloody cat ate our steak,' said Bert. 'Let's put him on the bathroom scales.'

Sure enough, the cat weighed in at exactly 4 lb. 'Just as we thought,' said Charlie, 'there's our steak, all right. *Now where's the flippin' cat*?'

From the personal column of a newspaper: 'Ex-London publican seeks widow with pub. Send photo of pub.'

Pub graffiti: IT WAS A WOMAN WHO DROVE ME TO DRINK AND I FORGOT TO WRITE AND THANK HER.

Doctor: 'Did you take your husband's temperature, like I told you?'

Wife: 'Yes, I did, doctor. I put it on his chest and it said *Very Dry*, so I brought him a pint of beer and he went back to work.'

This henpecked husband got back from the pub and announced: 'I'm fed up with married life. I'm going to join the Foreign Legion.'

'Well,' retorted his wife, 'don't come back in here treading sand all over the place!'

This Birmingham family took in a lodger. One night the husband came home early from the pub and caught him in bed with his wife.

'That's a fine way to repay our hospitality,' he cried. 'We've treated you like one of the family. *And stop doing that when I'm talking to you!*'

This punter gets home from the pub at 3 a.m. to be met by his wife in the hall. 'We've had a burglar while you were away boozing,' she sobs.

'Did he get anything?'

'I'll say – I thought he was you!'

How about the wife who suggested her alcoholic hubby leave his body to science? That way, she explained, it won't be completely wasted.

The couple were on their way to a cheese and wine party. 'Now, remember,' warned the wife, 'if it's a dull party – just leave it like that.'

'I thought you said, if I bought you a pint, you would tear a telephone directory in half?'

'That's right – page by page.'

Pub graffiti: IF YOU FEEL THE DRAUGHT, DON'T BE BITTER.

A fancy chap minced into the bar with this Doberman Pinscher and asked for a Scotch and soda.

'Sorry,' said the landlord, 'we don't serve your type in here.'

'You'd better,' warned the feller, 'or I'll set my dog on you.'

'You can do what you like,' said the barman, 'but I'm not giving you a drink.'

So the chap turned to the Doberman and shouted: 'Get him, boy!'

At which, the Doberman pinned the landlord against the wall and said: 'Woof, woof!'

Two punters in a pub. 'Did you hear that Willie taught his dog to eat when a bell rang?'

'Really?'

'Yes – he ate the Avon lady.'

News Flash: 'Four Scots arrested in Abu Dhabi are on their way home. They were accused of drinking alcohol, but released. The Justice Minister explained that his country respected the religious beliefs of other nations.'

Pub graffiti: DRINK MORE LIQUOR. WATER CAN KILL – REMEMBER THE FLOOD.

Then there was the feller who thought a herbacious border was a vegetarian lodger until he discovered Smirnoff.

A man goes into a pub with a fierce-looking Alsatian. 'You'd better leave that animal outside,' advised the barman.

Twenty minutes later, a woman rushes in and asks who owns the Alsatian.

'I do,' says the punter. 'What's the problem?'

'I've some bad news,' says the woman. 'My dog has killed your dog.'

'What kind of dog do you have?'

'A Chihuahua.'

'How did it manage to kill my Alsatian?'

'That's what I'm trying to tell you – it got stuck in its throat!'

How about the boozer who saw the sign 'Drink Canada Dry' – so he went.

A drunk was passing a garden, where a woman was grilling a chicken on a spit.

'Hey, missus,' he shouted, 'you'll never get a tune out of that – your bloody monkey's on fire!'

An Irishman put a parcel on the bar. 'What's that?' asked the barman.

'It's my lunch.'

'Is it tickin'?'

'No, it's turkey.'

Then there was the Scots tippler whose party piece was playing *Amazing Grace* on the breathalyser.

This drunk phones the police. 'I've been driving along the motorway (*hic!*), and I thought I'd let you know I've run over some bollards, knocked down an AA kiosk, and – '

'That's very interesting,' interrupts the policeman, 'and where exactly are you, sir?'

And the drunk replies: 'Wouldn't you like to know!'

'Can I get you a drink?' this chap asks the dolly bird in the pub.

'No, thanks, I don't drink,' she replies.

'Smoke?'

'I don't, thanks.'

'Game of darts, then?'

'I'm afraid I don't play.'

'Then can I see you home?'

'Very well.'

So they get to her house, and she opens the door. And there, lying in the hall, is a dead camel.

'Well,' says the girl, 'I never said I was tidy, did I?'

PubTalkPubTalkPubTalkPubTalkPubTalk

'Do you believe in clubs for women?'

'No – I always try kindess first.'

'As a golfer, I always go out in the low '70s.'

'Really?'

'Yes – if it's any colder, I stay home and watch TV.'

'Why are you putting your hand in the dog's mouth?'

'Putting it in? I'm trying to get it out!'

'My hubby wears the trousers in our house, but I tell him which ones to put on.'

'Did you say cold? Even the one-armed bandit had a glove on.'

'When a woman gets to fifty, you should be able to swop her for two twenty-fives.'

'The missus always has her own way. She even writes her diary three weeks ahead.'

'Has your wife learnt to drive the car yet?'

'Only in an advisory capacity.'

'I'm glad morning only comes once a day.'

A ventriloquist is telling Irish jokes at a pub talent night, when an Irishman stands up: 'You're making out we're all dumb and stupid. I ought to punch you on the nose.'

'I'm sorry, pal,' says the ventriloquist apologetically, 'I never – '

'Not you,' interrupts the Irishman, 'I'm talking to that little fella on your knee!'

This chap goes into a bar with a mongrel dog and says: 'This dog of mine understands every word I say. It's amazing.'

The regulars looked sceptical, so they have a whipround to disprove the point.

After raising £30, they approach the man to make a bet. 'Very well,' he said. 'If I tell my dog to do something and he obeys, I win the £30 – right?' The others agree.

So the chap goes over to the fireplace, throws the dog on to the blazing fire, and shouts: 'Rover – get off!'

On the loo wall of a pub: 'ARE YOU A MAN OR A MOUSE?' Below, someone has written: 'My wife is scared of mice.'

'Whatever time I get home, day or night, the missus always greets me with a kiss.'

'That's incredible. She must really love you.'

'No – she just wants to find out if I've been down at the pub.'

Pub graffiti: THERE NO ALCOHOL IN IRAN, BUT YOU CAN GET STONED ANY TIME.

Two old codgers in a pub. 'How did you get on at the doctor's, Fred?'

'I told him I wanted my sex urge lowered.'

'What did he say to that?'

'He reminded me I was eighty-three years old, and said it was all in my head.'

'How did you take that?'

'I said: "I know, doctor. I want it lowered." '

Hubby in pub: 'I'm just going to have an open sandwich, love — what are you just going to have?'

A man due to appear in court met a pal in a pub the night before, who advised: 'If you want to get off, just send the judge a couple of fresh salmon beforehand.'

Next morning, the man met his solicitor and told him of the conversation. 'On no account do anything like that,' warned the solicitor. 'We have a weak case, anyway, and an action like that would go against you.'

When the case came up, the chap won, to his solicitor's astonishment. 'I never thought we had a chance,' he told his client over a celebration pint. 'Did you really send the judge those salmon?'

'Yes,' came the reply, 'but I put the other party's name on them.'

'Excuse me, sir, can you direct me to the nearest boozer?'

'You're looking at him.'

This fella rushes into a bar. 'How tall is a penguin?' he asks the barman.

'Oh, about three feet.'

'Thank heavens for that — I thought I ran over a nun!'

'For twenty years, the wife and I were deliriously happy.'

'Then what happened?'

'We met each other.'

Two chaps in a pub. 'I've been feeling depressed all day,' says one.

'What's the problem?' asks the other.

'Well, back in 1965, I decided to murder the missus, but my solicitor talked me out of it. He said I'd get twenty years in jail.'

'Well?'

'All day I've been thinking ... today I'd be free!'

'I wasn't drunk, your honour. I was only drinking.'

'In that case, I'll give you thirty days in jail, instead of a month.'

Sign in country hotel: 'Ladies are requested not to have children in the cocktail lounge.'

Pub graffiti: IF LABOUR IS THE ANSWER, IT MUST HAVE BEEN A BLOODY STUPID QUESTION.

This commercial traveller was in a pub in Belfast. 'It's nice to be in a genuine Irish pub again,' he remarked, 'even to the sawdust bins in the corner.'

'Them's not sawdust bins, sir,' came the reply. 'Them's last night's furniture.'

How about the Aberdonian who always drinks with a friend?

That way, he's got someone to carry him home.

Thought for Today: Happiness is in cider all of us.

A punter came into the pub with a spaniel puppy under his arm.

'That's a nice pup,' remarked a pal.

'Yes, I got it for my missus.'

'By heck, I wish I could swop mine for one.'

Said a worried Archie in the pub: 'I've got a problem, Phil. This letter came the other day. It said: 'If you don't stop making love to my wife, I'm going to kill you.'

'So what's the problem?'

'It wasn't signed.'

Then there was the drinker who claimed his wife converted him to religion. He didn't know what Hell was till he married her.

Sean decided to set fire to his failing pub and collect the insurance. After he'd set it ablaze, he called the police and told them a gorilla had done it.

'Would you be able to recognize it again?' asked the copper.

'I can't be sure,' replied Sean. 'It was wearing a mask.'

'I drink three pints of Guinness every night for my insomnia.'

'Has it helped?'

'No, but now I don't mind staying awake so much.'

How about the man of eight-five who married a barmaid of nineteen? He had delusions of glandeur.

Then there was the pub landlord with a wooden leg. He used to make his own hops.

Man in pub: 'Take a look at this emerald ring I bought for the wife.'
'That isn't an emerald – an emerald's green.'
'Just wait till she wears it a while!'

And how about the tippler who died and left his wife a windfall? An apple.

'Mum, will you tell me a fairy story?'
'Better ask your father – I haven't heard any to beat the one he told me at three o'clock this morning.'

'What'll you have to drink?'
'A mother-in-law.'
'What's that?'
'Stout and bitter.'

Sad about the Glasgow man who fell into a vat of beer. He came to a bitter end.

A fella came into a pub and told his pal: 'I've a surprise for you – a spare ticket to see Shirley Bassey at the Festival Hall.'

'I don't want it,' replied his pal, knocking back yet another pint.

'You must be crazy,' said the fella. 'Shirley Bassey is the greatest singer in the world.'

'Like hell she is,' came the reply. 'I once saw a girl imitating her in a bar and she was terrible!'

Pub graffiti: PEOPLE IN GLASS HOUSES SHOULDN'T GET STONED.

Two drunks in a bar. 'Hey, Jimmy,' says one, 'I thought you were dead.'

'Not me, pal. I'm still around.'

'Then who the hell's funeral did I go to last October?'

It was a hot day, and this chap parked on a steep hill. Before locking the door, he ordered his dog to remain under the seat. 'Stay!' he commanded to an apparently empty car, as he made to walk away.

Whereupon a passing drunk remarked: 'Hey, pal – why don't you just put on the hand brake?'

Pub sign: 'All drinking water here is passed by the management.'

PubTalkPubTalkPubTalkPubTalkPubTalk

'The missus is unbearable, but that's her only fault.'

'Remember, two can live as cheaply as one.'
   'One *what*?'

'When did you first suspect your wife of cheating?'
   'When she got a gardener in – we've only got a window box.'

'My grandad lived to one-hundred-and-three and never used glasses.'
   'So what? Lots of people drink from the bottle.'

'I wanted to squander all my money, but the wife beat me to it.'

'She says she suffers from hallucinations, Jessie, but I think she's imagining it.'

151

'I bought the missus a foreign cookery book, and now she complains she can't get parts for the meals.'

'Narrow-minded? He can look through a keyhole with both eyes at the same time.'

'My man's one of the world's greatest lovers … and one day I'm gonna catch him at it.'

'The wife gets my shirts really white. Even when they're blue.'

After a lifetime of drinking, gambling and womanising, Sandy was on his deathbed. The minister was called to ease his way into the next world.

'The time has come,' he intoned, 'to renounce the Devil and all his works. Tell that Old Satan you want no part of him.'

Sandy made to sit up. 'Take it easy, reverend,' he implored. 'This isnae the time tae antagonise the chappie!'

Did you hear about the newly-formed Smokers' Anonymous?

Whenever a member is tempted to light a fag, he calls up a friend and they get drunk together.

Overheard in a bar.

1st drunk: 'How long have you believed in reincarnation?'

2nd drunk: 'Ever since I was a frog.'

After losing a bridge game, the wife glared at her husband.

'I had four aces and three kings,' she complained. 'What in the world did you open no trumps on?'

Replied the husband: 'Two jacks, two queens and four Martinis.'

Then there was the chap who drinks to forget, but never forgets to drink.

A salesman offered his best customer a litre bottle of White Horse whisky as a Christmas present.

'I'm sorry,' said the client, 'it's unethical and against my company's principles to accept gifts of any kind.'

'Very well,' said the salesman, 'what if I offer it to you at 50p for the bottle?'

'That's different,' replied the client. 'I'll take four.'

A man was admiring his neighbour's newly-painted house.

'You'd be surprised,' said the neighbour, 'how many gallons of beer it takes to paint a house of this size.'

Two brothers, identical twins, ordered drinks in a pub. A drunk sitting nearby took one look at them, shuddered, and ordered another Scotch.

'Take it easy, pal,' said one of the brothers. 'You're not seeing things. We happen to be identical twins.'

The drunk looked at them closely for a moment. 'All FOUR of you?' he asked.

A journalist asked this chap of one-hundred-and-five why he thought he'd lived so long. ' I attribute my long life to a couple of whiskies a day,' he replied.

'Nothing else?' inquired the journalist.

'Just one more thing – cancelling my voyage on the Titanic.'

How about the drunk who runs his wedding movie backwards so he can see himself walk out of church a free man?

'You're a fine friend,' Duggie chided Pat. 'Last night I was really drunk. I walked down the road, drinking in every pub I came to. Finally, I got into a fight and the police threw me into jail. I called your house, your job — all the places I could think of. Where the hell were you when I needed you?'

'With you,' replied Pat.

Definition of an Irish alcoholic: Someone who goes into a topless bar just to drink.

Jackie's car went out of control, knocked over a lamppost, and plunged straight through a plate glass window.

A policeman came on the scene. 'May I ask you if you have been drinking, sir?'

'What else?' replied Jackie. 'Nobody could drive that bad when they're sober!'

Man in pub: 'How's your missus getting on with her driving lessons?'

'Not bad ... the road is starting to turn when she does.'

Why does Guinness have a white head?
So you know which end to drink first.

A feller was enjoying a quiet pint, when Fred the barman asked him a riddle: 'My mother had a child. It wasn't my brother, it wasn't my sister. Who was it?'

The chap scratched his head. 'I give in,' he said finally.

'It's easy,' replied the barman. 'It's me, of course!'

When the punter got home, he tried the riddle on his wife: 'My mother had a child. It wasn't my brother, it wasn't my sister. Who was it?'

'Dunno,' said his wife.

'Easy,' came the reply. 'It's Fred the barman down at the pub!'

These twelve skinheads were crowding the bar. 'Give us thirteen pints,' orders one.

Said the barman: 'Excuse me for asking, but there's only twelve of you.'

Replied the skinhead: 'When I ask for thirteen pints, I *mean* thirteen pints – right?' So the barman serves up thirteen pints, and the skinheads march over to a table, where a little weedy guy is sitting on his own.

'Here you are, pal,' says the skinhead, 'have a pint on us. We like to buy a pint for a cripple.'

'That's nice of you, son, but I'm not a cripple.'

'You will be, chum, if you don't buy the next round!'

Old drinkers never die. They just get plastered.

Muldoon went to a psychiatrist. 'Every time I get drunk and sleep with strange women,' he explained, 'my conscience starts to bother me.'

'I see,' said the psychiatrist, 'so you'd like me to help you develop more will power ... make it stronger, in other words?'

'Oh, no,' protested Muldoon. 'I want you to *weaken* my conscience!'

At Hallowe'en, Jock and his pals dunked for apples in a bucket of Johnnie Walker whisky. Nobody won ... but you never saw such a gang of cheerful losers.

The new minister was delivering a sermon on the evils of drink. 'My friends,' he thundered, 'can anyone tell me what is worse than alcohol?'

And a drunken voice from the back shouted: 'Not having any!'

'There's many a slip between cup and lip,' said McDougall.

'That's why I always drink straight fae the bottle.'

Two drunks in a pub. 'The Government is clever,' said one. 'They raise the price of a drink, then make sure the country is in such a mess that you drink more.'

Two fellers in the pub were discussing predictions. 'According to a top scientist,' says one, 'the earth is going to explode in a billion years.'

The other chap's hand shook so violently he almost spilt his fifteenth pint. 'What did you just say?' he asked.

'I said a top scientist predicts the earth will blow up in a billion years.'

'That's better,' says the other with relief. 'I thought for a minute you said a *million* years!'

This mild-mannered chap came home from the pub and found his wife in bed with his best friend.

Spotting the man's umbrella in the corner, he seized it and smashed it into bits.

'Take that!' he murmured. 'And I hope it rains!'

A police car raced to a Cortina that had crashed into a lamp standard. 'Someone in this car is going to get done for drunk driving,' warned the sergeant.

And a chorus of boozy voices answered: 'How come, serge? We're all in the back seat!'

Joe was drinking heavily in the pub, when somebody yelled in: 'Hey, Joe – a feller's stealing your car!'

Joe staggered outside and raced down the road after the vehicle. A few minutes later, he wandered back into the bar.

'Did you catch him?' asked the barman.

'Not quite,' replied Joe, 'but I got his number!'

A copper arrested a chap for being drunk and disorderly and smoking downstairs in a bus.

'Can't you read, pal?' asked the copper, pointing to the NO SMOKING sign.

'No, I can't,' came the blurred reply.

'O.K. What's your name?'

The drunk mumbled something incomprehensible. 'Write it down,' ordered the cop, handing over his notebook.

The drunk scrawled an unreadable signature. 'What does that say?' asked the puzzled cop.

'Dunno,' replied the drunk. 'I told you I can't read.'

'I've just taken up jogging,' says this chap in the pub. 'It's said to add years to your life.'

'How do you feel?' asked a pal.

'Ten years older.'

'I don't enjoy drinking,' said Carruthers. 'It's just something to pass the time while I'm getting drunk.'

Man to his pal in a pub: 'The wife really enjoys the sales. She buys absolutely everything marked down.'

'Is that right?'

'Yes – only last week she came home with an escalator.'

Irish cocktail: A Guinness with a potato in it.

'Sure I smoke,' said Harry in the pub, 'but I never take more than one puff before throwing the cigarette away and stamping on it.'

'So what's your problem?' asked his pal.

'Cancer of the shoe.'

A feller in the pub was complaining he was

always tired. 'Why don't you go to the doctor?' suggested his mate.

So the chap went to the doctor, who asked him how often he had sex.

The feller replies: 'Monday, Tuesday, Wednesday, Thursday and Friday.'

Said the doctor: 'I think you'd better cut out Fridays.'

'Have a heart,' the punter replies, 'that's the only night I'm home!'

Going to a psychiatrist didn't cure Wally's drink problem.

He kept falling off the couch.

A fella was buying drinks for everyone in the bar after a big win at poker.

Said a pal: 'You seem to be very lucky at cards. How come you don't play the horses?'

'I don't get to deal the horses.'

Two drunks watched a well-heeled fella pushing a trolleyful of groceries out of a supermarket.

Says one to the other: 'How do you like that – spending all that money on food, when I bet he hasn't got a drop of booze in the house!'

This punter staggered home very late from the pub and told his wife he'd been out with his cousin.

'Liar!' she said. 'Your cousin and his wife were here all evening.'

'Look,' said the tippler, 'who are you going to believe – me or your own eyes?'

'What's that on your head, George – a hairpiece?'

'As a matter of fact, it is.'

'Fancy that – I would never have known.'

PubTalkPubTalkPubTalkPubTalkPubTalk

'I hear your lad got into college. What'll he be when he comes out?'

'Forty-five.'

'Arthur's a man of very few words, Ivy – all of them unrepeatable.'

'How are things, Fred?'

'Great – I've a wife and a cigarette lighter, and they both work.'

'The wife's TV dinners melt in the mouth.'
  'I wish mine would defrost them first, an' all.'

'These new shoes hurt.'
  'You've got them on the wrong feet.'
  'They're the only feet I have.'

'What's the simplest cure for double vision, Bob?'
  'Shut one eye.'

'Hey, Jimmy, what's Walter's last name?'
  'Walter who?'

'How many miles to the gallon do you get in your car?'
  'About ten – the missus gets the rest.'

A chap came home from the pub and found his wife in bed with another man. Instead of reading the Riot Act, the hubby says: 'Let's settle this in a civilized manner. How about playing a game of gin rummy to decide who gets the wife? If you win, I'll promise never to see her again.'
  'That's sporting of you,' said the other man, 'but why don't we play for a penny a point, just to make it interesting?'

This drunk accosted a chap in Watford High Street. 'Give us a handout,' he implored, 'I haven't had a bite for a week.'

'Don't worry,' replies the feller, 'it still tastes the same.'

Muldoon is a deep thinker, especially when he's half drunk. One night he asked his friend Hagan: 'Have you ever wondered why polar bears wear fur coats?'

'That's easy,' replied Hagan, 'because they'd looked damned silly in double-knits.'

'Doctor, my husband thinks he's an olive.'

'What makes you say that?'

'He keeps sticking his head in other people's Martinis.'

This punter in the pub was sobbing into his beer. 'What's the matter, pal?' asked the barman.

Replied the punter: 'I can't remember the name of the girl I'm trying to forget.'

This drunk was walking down the street with both ears blistered, when a pal stopped him and asked what happened.

'It was like this,' he explained. 'The wife left her hot iron by the phone when she left the room. The phone rang, and I picked up the iron by mistake.'

'But what about the *other* ear?' asked his mate.

'He called back!'

Car sticker: TRAINEE ALCOHOLIC.

On the way home one night, a drunk came on an amateur astronomer in his front garden, inspecting the heavens through his telescope.

Just as the drunk looked up, a shooting star flashed downwards.

' 'Struth,' said the drunk in amazement, 'you really are a crack shot!'

Then there was the landlady who was going to give a customer the usual ... till the landlord came in.

Two men in a pub. 'Do you think marriage is a lottery, Fred?'

'No, Charlie — in a lottery you have a chance.'

A drunk staggered into a phone box to phone a pal, put 10p in the box, and chattered on for forty-five minutes.

Coming out, he told a chap waiting outside: 'Hey, Jimmy, this phone's magic. You get forty-five minutes for only 10p.'

'I know,' replied the man. 'I've come to fix it.'

A feller in a pub wanted to go to the loo, so he left a note beside his pint: 'I've spat in this.'

When he got back, there was another note beside the pint: 'I've spat in it, too.'

'Mum, what's pop-art?'

'Why do you ask?'

'Well, that's what Dad always says when he's going to pop-art for a quick one down the pub.'

When several vats in an American brewery were struck by lightning, the beer in them was found to have improved considerably. This is believed to be the first recorded case of a storm actually brewing ...

Man to wife in pub: 'Of course I know what an erogenous zone is. I got booked for parking in one yesterday.'

'Do you believe in reincarnation?'
  'I suppose it's all right on the fruit salad.'

'Tight? She wouldn't even give a piece of her mind free.'

'They say a good woman is like a bottle of the finest wine.'
  'I know what you mean – you can't get the top off.'

'No, I don't wake up sleepy and irritable – I let her sleep in.'

'I hear you've bought a new car?'
  'Yeh – it's the only way to get the wife to belt up at the back.'

'The trouble with women, Bert, is that they're not human.'

'I thought I'd lost 195 lbs of ugly fat. Then the wife comes back.'

'That woman's got enough mouth for two sets of teeth.'

'My missus talks so much I get hoarse listening to her.'

'Unlucky? He broke his leg in an ear, nose and throat hospital.'

'He hasn't an enemy in the world, Margaret —
that's what I can't stand about him.'

'I'll say it was a posh pub — they served
Drambuie on draught.'

This fat feller went to see a phsychiatrist. 'The
reason you're so fat,' he announced, 'is that
your whole life is orientated towards eating
and drinking. You like parties for the punch
and the hors-d'oeuvres. A football match to
you means beer and hot dogs. Watching
television is a succession of booze and
snacks ... '
   'Just a minute,' interrupted the chappie,
'don't you serve anything during analysis?'

A punter told his two pals in the pub: 'After
the wife read *Double Trouble*, she had twins.'
'That's nothing,' said one. 'My missus read
The Three Musketeers and promptly had
triplets. Where are you off to, Jim?'

   And Jim replied: 'I've got to get home — I
left the wife reading *Ali Baba and the Forty
Thieves.*'

Police stopped a car near a pub at two in the morning and asked the driver where he was going.

'I'm on my way to a lecture,' he replied.

The sergeant asked where the lecture was being held, and the man gave an address identical to the one on his driving licence.

'And just who will be giving this lecture?' asked the sergeant.

The driver looked at him mournfully and said: 'My wife.'

Two men in a pub. 'Hey, Charlie – remember last time when I was broke and you helped me out, and I said I'd never forget you?'

'Yes?'

'Well, I'm broke again.'

Staggering into a bar, a drunk shouted 'Happy New Year, everyone!'

A chap next to him said: 'You idiot – it's the middle of June.'

'My God,' said the drunk, 'the wife'll kill me. I've never been *this* late before!'

Girl to girl in pub: 'When I turned down Albert, he went off on a drinking spree.'

'Well, he had to celebrate *some* way.'

Scene in a Dublin pub. The customers are sitting around drinking, and a dog is quietly chewing a bone in a corner.

Near closing time, the dog's master stands up and shouts 'Rover!'

The dog stands up, wags his tail ... and his hind leg drops off.

Archie's doctor told him to cut down on his boozing at the pub and just have a pint at home at meal times. Now his wife is run off her feet, making fifteen meals a day ...

A big chap goes up to the bar, slaps down his money, and roars: 'A pint for 10p – or else!' The barman gets the message, serves him his pint and takes the coin.

Whereupon a little feller, looking on, decides to follow suit. Slapping down his money, he shouts at the barman: 'A pint for 10p – or else!'

'Or else *what*?' snarls the barman.

'Or else a packet of crisps,' murmurs the wee man.

This drunk got run over by a mobile library. As he lay groaning in the road, the driver leaned out of his cab, put his finger to his lips, and said: '*Shhhhhhhhhhh*!'

'McDougall certainly knows how to put his drink away.'

'Aye, it's in the cupboard as soon as he sees visitors arrive.'

Then there was the tippler who tried to get a part in *Coronation Street*, because the cast were always in the Rover's Return.

A chap who'd had too much to drink stood on the promenade and gazed at the reflection of the moon on the sea.

'What's that down there?' he asked a passer-by.

'It's the moon.'

'Well ... how the hell did I get up here, then?'

This rabbit went into a bar for a pub lunch. 'Do you have any toasties?' he asked the barman. 'Ham, cheese or tomato,' the barman replied.

'I'll have a ham one and a pint of beer,' requested the rabbit.

When he'd finished this, he asked for a cheese toastie, and finally requested a tomato toastie.

When the rabbit finished all this, he dropped down dead.

That evening, the ghost of the rabbit

appeared, and the barman asked him what he had died of.

And the rabbit replied: 'Mixin Ma Toasties.'

When the astronaut opened a pub on the moon, why wasn't it a success?

It had no atmosphere.

A feller in a pub notices another drinker with a newt on his shoulder.

'Excuse me,' he said, 'but you have a newt on your shoulder.'

'Yes, as a matter of fact, it's my pet.'

'What do you call it?'

'Tiny.'

'Why Tiny?'

'Because it's my newt.'

A feller went into the pub and asked for a can of lager and a glass. Then he took a tin opener from his pocket, opened the can, and drank the lager.

'Why don't you use the ring opener?' asked the barman.

'Oh,' said the chap, 'I thought it was for people who didn't happen to have a tin opener in their pocket.'

Famous Last Words: 'This'll be the best home brew yet.'

At last!
THE OFFICIAL IRISH JOKE BOOK NO. 2

THE EAGERLY-AWAITED CLASSIC SEQUEL TO
BOOKS 1, 3, AND 4

Did you know about the Irish hammer thrower given
a dope test at the Olympics? He passed.

Or the sad fate of the Irish poultry farmer who went
broke giving away free-range eggs?

Did you hear about the groundsman of the shinty club
who thought he'd solve the drought problem by
diluting the water?

Or why Paddy decided to sell his passport? He was
going abroad.

At last! The Official Irish Joke Book No. 2 is here.

Futura Publications
Humour
0 7088 2669 5

THE BOOK OF EXCUSES

Gyles Brandreth

A COMPLETE GUIDE TO HOW TO COME UP WITH THE PERFECT EXCUSE!

Whoever you are — a child who hasn't done his homework, a husband who arrives home later than expected, a secretary who never gets to the office on time, a zookeeper who can't persuade his pandas to breed — you need an excuse.

They don't always need to be elaborate, but they always ought to be convincing — and with Gyles Brandreth's entertaining guidance and his selection of the most amazing real-life excuses ever known — they certainly will be!

From the government spokesman who excused the fact that Britain had been left behind in the race to the moon on the grounds that we led the world in sewage treatment . . .

. . . to the Unigate milkman who told an industrial tribunal that the reason he joined the housewife in her bath was to help her rinse her empties . . .

. . . to an unemployed accountant who, when asked in court whether he had sold a £3 bag of manure for £650, replied: 'Mark-ups are normal in any profession.'

THE BOOK OF EXCUSES MEANS YOU'LL NEVER HAVE TO SAY SORRY AGAIN!

Futura Publications
Humour
0 7088 2452 8

All Futura Books are available at your bookshop or newsagent, or can be ordered from the following address:
Futura Books, Cash Sales Department,
P.O. Box 11, Falmouth, Cornwall

Please send cheque or postal order (no currency), and allow 55p for postage and packing for the first book plus 22p for the second book and 14p for each additional book ordered up to a maximum charge of £1.75 in U.K.

Customers in Eire and B.F.P.O. please allow 55p for the first book, 22p for the second book plus 14p per copy for the next 7 books, thereafter 8p per book.

Overseas customers please allow £1.00 for postage and packing for the first book and 25p per copy for each additional book.